Melville's Moby-Dick:
A Jungian Commentary

". . . I shall follow the endless, winding way—
the flowing river in the cave of man."
Herman Melville, *Pierre*, Book V, Chapter 7

MELVILLE'S MOBY-DICK:

A JUNGIAN COMMENTARY

An American Nekyia.

Edward F. Edinger

A NEW DIRECTIONS BOOK

Most of the material in this volume first appeared, in somewhat different form, in *Quadrant*, the journal of the C. G. Jung Foundation for Analytical Psychology.

Manufactured in the United States of America
First published clothbound and as New Directions Paperbook 460 in 1978
Published simultaneously in Canada by McClelland & Stewart, Ltd.

Library of Congress Cataloging in Publication Data
Edinger, Edward F.
  Melville's Moby-Dick.
  (A New Directions Book)
  "Most of the material in this volume first appeared in somewhat different form in Quadrant."
  Bibliography: p. 144
  1. Melville, Herman, 1819–1891. Moby Dick.
I. Title.
PS2384.M62E3   813'.3   78–6146
ISBN 0–8112–0690–4
ISBN 0–8112–0691–2 pbk.

New Directions Books are published for James Laughlin
by New Directions Publishing Corporation,
333 Sixth Avenue, New York 10014

ACKNOWLEDGMENTS

Grateful acknowledgment is made for permission to reprint from the following copyrighted sources: for an excerpt from *The Day Lincoln Was Shot* by Jim Bishop (Copyright © 1955 by Jim Bishop), reprinted by permission of Harper & Row Publishers, Inc., and International Creative Management; for a selection from *The Divine Comedy* by Dante, translated by Lawrence Grant White (Copyright 1948 by Pantheon Books, Inc.), reprinted by permission of Pantheon Books, A Division of Random House, Inc.; for excerpts from "The Waste Land" and "The Hollow Men" in *Collected Poems 1909-1962* by T. S. Eliot (Copyright 1936 by Harcourt Brace Jovanovich, Inc.; Copyright © 1963, 1964 by T. S. Eliot); reprinted by permission of Harcourt Brace Jovanovich, Inc., and Faber and Faber, Ltd.; for a selection from *Faust* by Johann Wolfgang von Goethe, translated by Louis MacNeice (Copyright 1951 by Louis MacNeice), reprinted by permission of Oxford University Press, and Faber and Faber, Ltd.; for a selection from *Faust, Part 1* by Johann Wolfgang von Goethe, translated by George Madison Priest (Copyright 1941, renewed 1969 by Alfred A. Knopf, Inc.), reprinted by permission of Alfred A. Knopf, Inc.; for the sonnet "Design" from *The Poetry of Robert Frost*, edited by Edward Connery Lathem (Copyright 1936 by Robert Frost; Copyright © 1964 by Lesley Frost Ballantine; Copyright © 1969 by Holt, Rinehart and Winston), reprinted by permission of Holt, Rinehart and Winston, Publishers, and Jonathan Cape, Ltd.; for an excerpt from *The Collected Works of C. G. Jung*, translated by R. F. C. Hull, Bollingen Series XX, Vol. 9, I, *The Archetypes and the Collective Unconscious* (Copyright © 1959, 1969 by Princeton University Press), reprinted by permission of Princeton University Press; for a passage from *Memories, Dreams, Reflections* by C. G. Jung, recorded and edited by Aniela Jaffe, translated by Richard and Clara Winston (Copyright © 1962, 1963 by Random House, Inc.), reprinted by permission of Pantheon Books, A Division of Random House.

NOTE: The Greek word *NEKYIA* [nek-ee-eé-ah] has been suggested by Jung as a term for the "descent to the underworld." He writes, "*Nekyia* . . . , the title of the eleventh book of the Odyssey, is the sacrifice to the dead for conjuring up the departed from Hades. *Nekyia* is therefore an apt designation for the 'journey to Hades,' the descent into the land of the dead. . . . Typical examples are the *Divine Comedy*, the classical *Walpurgisnacht* in *Faust*, the apocryphal accounts of Christ's descent into hell, etc." [*Psychology and Alchemy*, CW, 12, par. 61, n.2.]

CONTENTS

1   *Introduction*   1
2   *Melville the Man*   6
3   *Ishmael, the Alienated One*   15
4   *Queegqueg, the Primitive Shadow*   24
5   *The Sign of Jonah*   36
6   *The Nekyia Begins*   42
7   *Captain Ahab*   49
8   *Ahab and Mythology*   61
9   *The Meaning of the Whale*   73
10   *The Whiteness of the Whale*   80
11   *The Whale as Sphinx and Medusa*   89
12   *Fedallah, the Avenging Angel*   97
13   *Linked Analogies*   102
14   *The Pact with the Devil*   111
15   *Encounter with Numinosum*   120
16   *Transformation*   131
17   *Death and Rebirth*   137
    Bibliography   144
    Glossary   147

To Frances

1 INTRODUCTION

THIS ESSAY is a psychological study of Melville's *Moby-Dick*. I shall approach the novel as a psychological document, a record in symbolic imagery of an intense inner experience—as though it were a dream which needs interpretation and elaboration of its images for their meaning to emerge fully. I shall not explore to what extent Melville was conscious of the general or the personal implications of his own symbols. Whether he was or was not is irrelevant to our purpose and, from such a distance, would be impossible to determine. As Henry A. Murray has rightly said, "It would . . . be well if critics were protected from the mistake of dealing with Melville's thought on a rational level as if he had arrived at his conclusions by logical induction after an impartial survey of the universe."[1] We can only be sure that there is much more in *Moby-Dick* than Melville realized or consciously intended.

I hope in this undertaking to serve three ends: first, to elucidate the psychological significance of *Moby-Dick;* second, to demonstrate the methods of analytical psychology in dealing with symbolic forms; and third, to present the basic orientation, or *Weltanschauung*, which underlies the therapeutic approach of analytical psychology.

In general there are two basic and contrasting procedures of psychological interpretation. The first and by far the more common procedure is to consider the imagery of dream, phantasy, or work of art as a secondary derivation of personal experiences. This interpretation reduces the images of the imagination to the personal experiences that supposedly evoked them. The "meaning" of the image is thought to be found by tracing its origin back to its source in the concrete events of the individual life. Thus, in this approach, the

---

[1] Henry A. Murray, "Introduction," *Pierre* (New York: Hendricks House, 1949), p. xvii.

psyche and its imaginative function are secondary to and derivative from factual life experience, which is the primary datum containing no prior meaningfulness.

The second, less frequent procedure is to consider the imaginative images as primary entities in their own right that convey the meaning of the experience to which they refer. It may even seem in some cases that the latent, a priori image causes the concrete, personal experience, rather than the experience being the cause of the image. Thus the psyche, the imagination, and the spirit are the primary data existing prior to, and indeed determining, personal experience. From this viewpoint, the meaning of the factual experience is interpreted through the images it evokes, whereas from the personalistic viewpoint the "meaning" of the image is thought to be found when it has been interpreted as deriving from its associated experience.

These two modes of psychological interpretation are both valid, in fact they complement one another. The first, which I call the personal interpretation, considers the psyche as caused by experience; it is based on a causalistic theory. The second, which I refer to as the archetypal interpretation, considers the psyche as an a priori entelechy; hence it is based on a teleological hypothesis. I shall attempt to use both these modes of interpretation in the examination of *Moby-Dick*, although their combination in practice requires the sacrifice of consistency and the enduring of a paradox.

It is by no means unanimously agreed that psychology properly can offer interpretations of works of art. Much of the resistance to the psychological study of art can be attributed to the exclusive use of the personal mode of interpretation, which attempts to fit deep and meaningful images into narrowly reductive and depreciatory formulae. Such one-sided "interpretations," because of their patent inadequacy to the subject matter, have tended to discredit the whole psychological approach to art. One psychoanalyst who is also a Melville scholar has put it this way:

> The habit of a psychologist is to break down the structure of each personality he studies into elements, and so in a few strokes to bring to earth whatever merit that structure, as a structure, may possess. Furthermore . . . the technical terms for the majority of these elements have derogatory connotations. Consequently, it is difficult to open one's professional mouth without disparaging a fellow-being.[2]

[2] Henry A. Murray, "In Nomine Diaboli," *Moby-Dick Centennial Essays* (Dallas: Southern Methodist University Press, 1953), p. 4.

In spite of obvious misuses of limited and inadequate psychological theories, it must be maintained on principle that the science of psychology includes in its proper subject matter the study of works of art. For, as C. G. Jung has said, "the human psyche is the womb of all the arts and sciences."[3] If the application of a psychological theory to a work of art makes a travesty of the artistic creation, so much the worse for the theory. It will have been proved inadequate to the depth and breadth of the human soul. In my opinion, the only psychological theory that comes even close to describing the human psyche in its true dimensions is that of Jung.

The major defect in most psychological interpretations of art and literature is that they have no understanding of the transpersonal layer of the psyche, variously called the collective unconscious, the objective psyche, or the archetypal psyche. Lacking this crucial feature, such interpretations can do no more than relate the contents of the work of art to the personal psychology of the artist. This personal mode of interpretation has a partial validity, but by itself creates a caricature that neglects the fundamental *raison d'être* of both art and artist. Rather than being an expression of the artist's personal neurosis, a great work of art is a self-revelation of the transpersonal objective psyche which speaks potentially to all men. Artistic creation, including philosophy and scientific theories, as well as literature and the visual arts, is inner vision incarnate. It is the visible evidence of the human acculturating process. Artistic creations perform for society much the same function that dreams perform for the individual. They are the mirror that reveals to us what we really are. Dreams reveal to the individual the dynamics of his personal destiny. Art makes manifest the collective *Zeitgeist* of society. In the case of the true artist these two functions become one. The individual artist suffers the fate of society, and his personal dreams and visions become identical with the expressions of the transpersonal world spirit.

If this be true, it is small wonder that an artist usually has a disturbed and often tragic personal life. It is not so much that his personal life explains his art; it is rather that his function as artist explains his personal life. The collective, objective psyche has commandeered him to make of him its mouthpiece. He has little to say in the matter.

---

[3] C. G. Jung, *The Spirit in Man, Art, and Literature*, CW 15 (Princeton, N.J.: Princeton University Press, 1966), par. 133.

The gift is thrust upon him, and yet he "must pay dearly for the divine gift of the creative fire."[4] The artist must function through his own personality, which necessarily includes his personal complexes and traumata. So it is legitimate to observe and discuss the effects of these personal complexes and traumata in his artistic work. However,

> The essence of a work of art is not to be found in the personal idiosyncrasies that creep into it—indeed, the more there are of them, the less it is a work of art—but in its rising above the personal and speaking from the mind and heart of the artist to the mind and heart of mankind.[5]

Many people consider *Moby-Dick* to be the greatest American novel. Certainly there is none to which could be applied more aptly Milton's statement that "a good book is the precious life blood of a master spirit." This book is palpitatingly alive. It is awesome in the intensity of the depths it reveals. Perhaps this is why it was largely misunderstood and neglected during Melville's lifetime. But collective consciousness has changed considerably in a hundred years. We have grown up to Melville. The problems he explored so deeply we now recognize as our problems.

Modern depth psychology is laying the foundations for a reliable *science of images*. The human imagination is now in the process of being studied by the same objective, empirical attitude applied previously to anatomy and physiology. Heretofore such a science has not been possible because, with isolated exceptions, man has not been able to separate his perceiving consciousness, the ego, from the autonomous images that rise up within him. Because there is a powerful tendency for the ego to identify with emerging images of the archetypal psyche, we have had many religious and philosophical dogmas but no science of archetypal images.

Until recently, the "eternal images" of the soul have been contained in the prevailing symbol-systems of organized religion. As traditional religion lost its capacity to carry living meaning, man was left without a containing vessel for the transpersonal symbols. This situation has had a two-fold effect. On the one hand, it has left countless people cut off from the roots of their being, feeling alone and helpless in an alien universe; on the other hand, the decline of

4 Ibid., par. 158.
5 Ibid., par. 156.

religion can be seen as a withdrawal of projections, which although it deprives heaven of its deity immensely enriches the inner world of man; indeed, it is a necessary precondition for the emergence of the science of depth psychology. There can be no scientific approach to the depths of the psyche as long as the contents of these depths are projected into an external system, such as a religious or philosophic creed. The death of religion gives birth to psychology, and the world-phoenix renews itself.

Moby-Dick is a product of this transition process in the collective psyche. It was written out of Melville's personal experience of simultaneously losing religious projections and discovering the transpersonal contents of the unconscious. It describes symbolically the stormy process of spiritual transition which Melville experienced; it also is a document of our civilization in transition. What Harold C. Goddard said so aptly about Shakespeare applies also to *Moby-Dick*. "Ours is a time that would have sent the Greeks to their oracles. We fail at our peril to consult our own."[6]

We can thus begin our examination of this greatest product of the American imagination with the assurance that it speaks to the modern mind with profound pertinence.

A word should be said about the psychological method used in this study. The psychological method differs from the literary or scholarly method. The former is not particularly interested in locating the literary or cultural sources of a theme or image; rather, it takes its subject—*Moby-Dick* in this case—as a manifestation of the psyche and is concerned to understand the *psyche* through a study of its manifestations. It is a strictly empirical and phenomenological method which assumes the work of art to be a natural organism, a living psychic product of the autonomous imagination, and not a deliberate contrivance of the conscious will.

In what follows I shall elaborate the archetypal aspects of *Moby-Dick* by amplifying them with many Biblical and mythological parallels, most of which have been previously demonstrated by various Melville scholars.[7] If I fail to acknowledge adequately this previ-

---

[6] Harold C. Goddard, *The Meaning of Shakespeare* (Chicago: University of Chicago Press, 1951), p. v.

[7] See especially Nathalia Wright, *Melville's Use of the Bible* (New York: Octagon Books reprint, 1974), and Gerard M. Sweeney, *Melville's Use of Classical Mythology* (Amsterdam: Rodopi N.V., 1975). Also to be mentioned

ous scholarly work it is in order not to blur my method. I am not a scholar but a depth psychotherapist. This essay is an effort not so much to understand Melville as to understand the psyche, especially the collective psyche, through the genius of Melville's imagination.

is Richard Slotkin's "*Moby-Dick*: The American National Epic," which applies Jungian terminology if not method to *Moby-Dick*, in Richard Slotkin, *Regeneration Through Violence: The Mythology of the American Frontier, 1600–1860* (Middleton, Conn.: Wesleyan University Press, 1973), pp. 539–50. An initial attempt to view Melville's total work in terms of Jungian concepts is found in Martin Leonard Pops, *The Melville Archetype* (Kent, Ohio: The Kent State University Press, 1970).

2 MELVILLE THE MAN

HERMAN MELVILLE was born on August 1, 1819, in New York City, the third of eight children and the second son. Both sides of his family were notable and had played important parts in the American Revolution. His father's side, originally Scots with connections in the peerage, were Boston merchants. As a memento of Grandfather Melville's participation in the Boston Tea Party of 1773, his descendants for years preserved a vial of tea leaves gathered from his boots on that night. His mother's family, the Gansevoorts of Albany, were Dutch brewers who had settled in Albany in the seventeenth century, rapidly achieving the status of landed gentry. On their side the outstanding ancestor was Herman's grandfather, General Peter Gansevoort, a hero of the Revolution, who had held Fort Stanwix against the British when they were marching down the Mohawk Valley to join forces with Burgoyne. The Gansevoorts were stolid, stable, eminent, prosperous people; the Melvilles were somewhat less successful materially, possessing an unpredictable, erratic, mercurial strain. Herman inherited the opposing tendencies of both sides.

His father, Allan Melville, a merchant and importer dealing chiefly in French goods, seems to have been socially charming and sensitive, but basically weak, with a long-standing financial and psychological dependence on his father and, more especially, on his wife's brother. There are definite indications that Allan Melville's sons may have found a more substantial father experience with their maternal uncle, Peter Gansevoort. There are also suggestions that the uncle actually wooed the sons' affection and respect away from their father, although evidence concerning Herman's early relation to his father is not clear. Allan Melville was apparently erratic and unrealistic in practical affairs. He seems to have been a man who constantly lived beyond his means, buoyed up by a wishful optimism, continually expecting a great windfall to be just around the corner. At the same time that he was borrowing money for business needs, he was trying to fulfill his wife's social ambitions by moving to larger and more expensive houses. Eventually, when the bubble burst, Melville's father suffered a total financial and psychological collapse.

There is ample evidence concerning Melville's relation to his mother, Maria. The haughty, possessive Mrs. Glendinning in Melville's novel *Pierre* surely includes many of his mother's characteristics. This novel and such passages from *Redburn* as, "the name of mother was the centre of all my heart's finest feelings,"[1] indicate that, during one phase at least, Melville was very attached to his mother. There is much evidence, however, that he felt his love was not reciprocated. In his old age, Melville once remarked to his niece that his mother "hated him."[2] Apparently the older son, Gansevoort, who carried the mother's maiden name, was distinctly her favorite. In a late poem, Melville writes of a mother who favored her older son against the younger:

> I made the junior feel his place,
> Subserve the senior, love him, too;
> And sooth he does, and that's his saving grace.
> But me the meek one never can serve,
> Not he, he lacks the quality keen
> To make the mother through the son
> An envied dame of power, a social queen.[3]

If these verses are not an accurate picture of Melville's actual mother, they express his subjective experience of her, as well as of his relation to his older brother.

It is my conclusion that Maria Melville never committed herself emotionally to her husband, but remained primarily attached to

---

[1] Newton Arvin, *Herman Melville* (New York: William Sloane Associates, 1950), p. 19.
[2] Ibid., p. 30.
[3] Herman Melville, "Timolean," *Collected Poems* (Chicago: Packard & Co., Hendricks House, 1947), p. 211.

the Gansevoort family, especially to her competent, accomplished brother. This circumstance compounded the effects of Allan's inherent weakness, making the psychic atmosphere of Melville's family that of a matriarchy in which the mother is the central figure and the masculine authority resides not with the father but with the maternal uncle.

Since in adult life Melville had such a marked religious preoccupation, the religious background of his family is particularly important. "The Calvinistic tradition had been established in both sides of the family generations before Melville was born."[4] Both his mother and father had strong religious convictions, expressed frequently in their letters. His father could write, "that divine first cause, who always moulds events to subserve the purposes of mercy and wisdom, often subjects poor human nature to the severest trials, that he may better display his sovereign power."[5] Similarly, his mother wrote, "The ways of Providence are indeed inscrutable and past finding out, but I am one of those who cling to the belief that somehow these mysterious dispensations will seem right to us, and 'at eventide there shall be light.' "[6] Her reaction to her husband's mental breakdown was, "God moves in a misterious way."[7] Despite its predestinarian harshness, the Calvinistic mythology does express forcefully the psychological truth that a transpersonal image of meaning (God) lies behind events. This assumption, held by both Melville's parents, permeated the psychic atmosphere in which he spent his childhood.

The first eleven years of Herman's life were apparently secure and relatively happy ones. There were long vacations during the summer, in Albany or Boston; there was a fine home to live in, probably unclouded by any awareness of the gathering storm. The storm broke, however, when Herman was eleven. Abruptly, his father went bankrupt, losing everything he had. The family left New York and retreated to the protective shadow of the Gansevoort family in Albany. Allan Melville attempted to carry on by entering a fur company there, but his spirit was broken. Within a year he had a

4 William Braswell, *Melville's Religious Thought* (New York: Pageant Books, 1959), p. 4.
5 Ibid., p. 5.
6 Ibid., p. 8.
7 Jay Leyda, *The Melville Log* (New York: Harcourt Brace & Co., 1951), i, p. 51.

complete mental breakdown. A few days before his psychic collapse, he marked in his Bible, Psalms 55:4–5:

> My heart is sore pained within me: and the terrors of death are fallen upon me. Fearfulness and trembling are come upon me and horror hath overwhelmed me.[8]

This state of mind heralded an overt psychosis, and in little more than two weeks, at the age of forty-nine, Allan Melville was dead. Herman certainly experienced the full impact of his father's fatal encounter with darkness, but was not old enough to assimilate the experience. It was, without doubt, a crucial trauma to him. Its effects, which he carried for the rest of his life, show up in much of his later writings. Abruptly his life was totally changed. At the age of twelve he was obliged to stop his education and go to work. For the next three or four years he held various clerical jobs and worked in the summers on an uncle's farm in Pittsfield. After a brief period as a student in the Albany Classical School, at eighteen he worked as a grade school teacher in a rural school near Pittsfield. This lasted only one semester. The following year he took a course in surveying and engineering, hoping to get a job with the Erie Canal. The job failed to materialize. Unable to get his bearings, not knowing what to do, in 1839, at the age of twenty, he signed up as a common seaman on a merchant vessel sailing for Liverpool. His experiences during this voyage he later used in his novel *Redburn*. He was back in four months, still not knowing what to do with his life. Again he tried teaching in a small village in upstate New York. But he was not paid his salary and left. He looked for a job in New York City without success. Finally, in December 1840, when he was twenty-one, he signed up for a four-year voyage on a whaling ship. One other factor may have contributed to Melville's taking to the sea. Frances G. Wickes has said that Melville was in love with her grandmother, Mary Eleanor Parmelee, who was committed to another man. This frustrated love affair, which took place sometime before Melville left for the South Seas, may have had some influence on his going.[9]

As Melville wrote in *Moby-Dick*, "a whaling ship was my Yale college and my Harvard." While other future writers were complet-

[8] Ibid.
[9] Eleanor Metcalf, *Herman Melville* (Cambridge, Mass.: Harvard University Press, 1953), p. 23.

ing their education, living with their intellectual equals, Melville was at sea, a common sailor, "washing down decks, reefing stunsails, standing mastheads, and generally rubbing shoulders with the brutalized, exploited, and mostly illiterate seamen."[10] Here is a second major trauma. From a cultivated, genteel environment, Melville was suddenly plunged, unprepared, into the coarse, brutal life of the sea. No wonder he developed a lifetime preoccupation with the antithesis between good and evil! Most of us are spared the tension of such extreme opposites. Yet, suffering the raw realities of life in place of the intellectual stereotypes of academic education probably deepened his capacity to see and feel and surely was necessary to the molding of his genius.

After a year and a half at sea, the whaler stopped briefly at the Marquesas Islands. Apparently unable to tolerate any more, Melville deserted ship with a friend. They made their way into the interior and became captive guests of the cannibal natives, as Melville described in his first book, *Typee*. After a few weeks he escaped, signed on another whaler going to Tahiti, and after many further adventures, which appeared fictionally in *Omoo*, found himself a sailor in the U.S. Navy aboard a man-o'-war, which we can read about in *White Jacket*. At last, almost four years after embarking on the whaleship, he landed in Boston, was discharged from the Navy, and returned home.

The experience of the primitive, idyllic, as yet unspoiled life of the South Sea islands was obviously another important influence on Melville's psychological development. The natives of the Marquesas in many ways lived in the paradise state of Adam before the Fall—before instinct and spirit were wrenched apart and turned into deadly enemies in the human psyche. Here sexuality was free and uninhibited; here Melville probably had his first sexual experience; and here he met a precursor of Queequeg, the noble savage in *Moby-Dick*. In *Typee* Melville wrote,

> . . . the Polynesian savage, surrounded by all the luxurious provisions of nature, enjoyed an infinitely happier, though certainly a less intellectual existence, than the self-complacent European. . . .
> In a primitive state of society, the enjoyments of life, though few and simple, are spread over a great extent, and are unalloyed; but

[10] Arvin, *op. cit.*, p. 37.

Civilization, for every advantage she imparts, holds a hundred evils in reserve;—the heart burnings, the jealousies, the social rivalries, the family dissensions, and the thousand self-inflicted discomforts of refined life, which make up in units the swelling aggregate of human misery, are unknown among these unsophisticated people. . . .

The term "Savage" is, I conceive, often misapplied, and indeed when I consider the vices, cruelties, and enormities of every kind that spring up in the tainted atmosphere of a feverish civilization, I am inclined to think that so far as the relative wickedness of the parties is concerned, four or five Marquesan Islanders sent to the United States as missionaries might be quite as useful as an equal number of Americans dispatched to the Islands in a similar capacity.[11]

At the conclusion of his whaling voyage Melville was twenty-five years old. In a letter to Hawthorne, seven years later, he wrote,

Until I was twenty-five, I had no development at all. From my twenty-fifth year I date my life. Three weeks have scarcely passed at any time between then and now, that I have not unfolded within myself."[12]

What had Melville been doing during those seven years of growth? The answer is, writing. From age twenty-five to thirty-two, he completed six books, the last one his masterpiece, *Moby-Dick*. Though all six of these books drew heavily on his experience at sea, it was the first, *Typee*, describing his life among the Marquesan natives, that won him overnight literary fame. His subsequent books received less notice or approval. Even *Moby-Dick*, while it received some good reviews, generally drew reactions similar to that in the London *Athenaeum*:

Melville must be henceforth numbered in the company of the incorrigibles, who occasionally tantalize us with indication of genius, while they constantly summon us to endorse monstrosities, carelessness, and other such harassing manifestations of bad taste as daring or disordered ingenuity can devise. . . . Mr. Melville has to thank himself only if his horrors and his heroics are flung aside by the general reader, as so much trash belonging to the worst school of Bedlam literature.[13]

Melville was definitely hurt by this kind of hostility, but another

---

[11] Herman Melville, *Typee* (New York: New American Library, 1964), p. 145f.
[12] Metcalf, *op. cit.*, p. 110.
[13] Leyda, *op. cit.*, p. 430f.

event, which occurred while he was writing *Moby-Dick*, was very helpful in bearing such hurts: he met Nathaniel Hawthorne. Melville's reaction was immediate and intense. It can only be described as a spiritual love affair, or, to use a psychological term, a transference. Being fifteen years older than Melville, Hawthorne undoubtedly carried some of the meaning of the missing father experience. Also, Melville projected onto Hawthorne his own emerging capacities for greatness. Much of his extravagant praise of his friend actually was more applicable to himself. The depth of his feeling is expressed in his reply to Hawthorne's letter complimenting him on *Moby-Dick*.

> Your letter was handed me last night on the road going to Mr. Morehead's, and I read it there. Had I been at home, I would have sat down at once and answered it. In me divine magnanimities are spontaneous and instantaneous—catch them while you can. The world goes round and the other side comes up. So now I can't write what I felt. But I felt pantheistic then—your heart beat in my ribs and mine in yours, and both in God's. A sense of unspeakable security is in me this moment on account of your having understood the book. . . . Whence came you, Hawthorne? By what right do you drink from my flagon of life? And when I put it to my lips—lo, they are yours and not mine. I feel that the Godhead is broken up like the bread at the Supper, and that we are the pieces. Hence this infinite fraternity of feeling.[14]

Hawthorne of course could not live up to such an intense transference. As with all powerful projections, it came with a possessiveness which provoked from its object a protective withdrawal. Hawthorne, a shy, introverted man, remained friendly, but did not share Melville's emotional involvement. As the friendship cooled, feeling the inevitable rebuff which excessive expectation brings, Melville was thrown back on himself. Many years later, following Hawthorne's death, Melville wrote this poem:

> To have known him, to have loved him
>   After loneness long;
> And then to be estranged in life,
>   And neither in the wrong;
> And now for death to set his seal—
>   Ease me, a little ease, my song!
> By wintry hills his hermit-mound

14 Metcalf, *op. cit.*, p. 128f.

The sheeted snow-drifts drape,
And houseless there the snow-bird flits
Beneath the fir-trees' crape:
Glazed now with ice the cloistral vine
That hid the shyest grape.[15]

In 1847, at the age of twenty-eight, Melville married Elizabeth
Shaw, daughter of a close family friend, Judge Lemuel Shaw of Boston. It is difficult to resist the impression that this marriage was motivated more by desire for a father than for a wife. Judge Shaw had
been a good friend of Allan Melville, was very helpful to Maria
when she was first widowed, and turned out to be a most kind and
generous father-in-law, buying Herman and Elizabeth a home and
later financing his son-in-law's journey to the Near East. The marriage seems to have been a difficult, problematical one. His attraction
to Elizabeth, a childhood family friend, was apparently more a matter of security than of passion. Perhaps it is significant that when
their second son's birth certificate was filled out, the name of the infant's mother was mistakenly written as Maria instead of Elizabeth.[16]

Undoubtedly, Melville was a difficult man to live with. Like his
fictional figure Ahab, he was gifted with the high perception, but
lacked the low, enjoying power. He was frequently moody and
withdrawn. On the evidence of his wife's letters, he was such a cause
of apprehension to her that at one period she feared for his sanity.
Melville's relation to the personal, practical aspects of life was always
poor. Without his wife's devoted care and the generous material assistance of her father, he probably could not have survived. These
two must share in the credit for the accomplishments of his genius.

Shortly after finishing *Moby-Dick*, Melville started another novel,
Pierre, which although interesting from the psychological standpoint
is less successful as a work of art. In general, it reproduces in personal
imagery the same psychological content that *Moby-Dick* expresses
in archetypal images. This means that the personal problems under-
lying both books were coming closer to consciousness. During the
next twelve years, from 1853 to 1865 (age thirty-four to forty-six),
Melville went through a period of extreme psychic distress and reorientation. His mental and physical health were in jeopardy, and

[15] "Monody," *Collected Poems*, p. 228f.
[16] Leyda, *op. cit.*, p. 430.

at times he was close to psychosis or suicide. During this period he was apparently living through the events that had been foreshadowed symbolically in *Moby-Dick*. He was entering the years Jung has described as the second half of life, requiring a major psychic reorientation and the development of a religious attitude. Coincidentally, Melville's period of stormy transition paralleled approximately the national tension that built up during the 1850s and culminated in the chaotic violence of the Civil War. By the end of the war, Melville's condition had stabilized. In 1866, he finally found steady, remunerative employment as a customs inspector for the Port of New York, the job he held for nineteen years until retirement at the age of sixty-six.

In spite of a regular job, Melville continued to write, turning increasingly to poetry. In addition to many incidental poems, he produced *Clarel*, a weighty, religious-philosophical poem, which derived its setting from his journey to the Holy Land in 1856–57. This work, long, difficult, and immensely rich in content, has yet to receive due recognition.

Melville's life continued to be dogged by tragedy. In 1867, his oldest son, Malcolm, died at the age of eighteen of a self-inflicted gunshot wound. His younger son, Stanwix, never found his place in life, but roamed about erratically trying first one thing and then another, finally dying of tuberculosis at the age of thirty-five. Others close to Melville had to pay the price for his genius. But, like Ishmael in *Moby-Dick*, Melville survived. Although customs inspector was a lowly position for a man of his talents, he did manage to bridge the gap between the opposites of his high creative capacities and the practical realities of material existence. His last work, *Billy Budd*, finished shortly before his death at seventy-two, demonstrates that a reconciliation was finally reached at the end of his "earthquake life."

Melville died in obscurity. The obituaries spoke of him as "a once popular author" whose best work was *Typee*.[17] By the middle of the twentieth century, however, it was beginning to dawn on Americans that Herman Melville is the greatest literary genius our country has yet produced.

[17] Ibid., p. 836f.

3 ISHMAEL, THE ALIENATED ONE

Moby-Dick BEGINS with the striking sentence, "Call me Ishmael," setting the theme of all that follows. We are immediately confronted with the Biblical figure of the rejected outcast, the alienated man.

At the beginning of Judaic mythical history stands the figure of Abraham, the progenitor of the Jews. Like Adam before him, Abraham had two sons—Isaac, the legitimate, accepted one, and Ishmael, the illegitimate, the rejected one. In the sixteenth chapter of Genesis, the angel of the Lord speaks to Hagar, saying,

> Behold, you are with child, and shall bear a son; you shall call his name Ishmael [literally, "God hears"]; because the Lord has given heed to your affliction. He shall be a wild ass of a man, his hand against every man and every man's hand against him, and he shall dwell over against all his kinsmen.*

Following Isaac's birth, Ishmael and his mother, Hagar, were cast into the wilderness to die. God preserved Ishmael, who, according to tradition, fathered the Muslim peoples. Thus, at the very outset, the seed of Abraham was split into two streams, into a pair of opposites. To Isaac and Judeo-Christianity, Ishmael is the adversary, the opposing alternative which must be rejected and repressed. But to himself, Ishmael is the rejected orphan who through no fault of his own has been cruelly cast out and condemned to wander beyond the pale. Ishmael is, therefore, the prototype of the alienated man, the outsider who feels he has no place in the nature of things.

Melville's other writings show that he was preoccupied throughout his life with the figure of Ishmael, the orphan, the child who was bitterly hurt. In *Mardi* he writes, "sailors are mostly foundlings and castaways and carry all their kith and kin in their arms and their legs," and in *Redburn*, "at last I found myself a sort of Ishmael in the ship, without a single friend or companion."[1] In *Pierre*, after a shocking experience the hero

* Unless otherwise noted, all Biblical quotes are from the Revised Standard Version.
[1] Herman Melville, *Redburn* (Garden City, N.Y.: Doubleday & Co., 1957), p. 60.

felt that deep in him lurked a divine unidentifiableness, that owned no earthly kith or kin. Yet was this feeling entirely lonesome, and orphanlike. Fain, then, for one moment, would he have recalled the thousand sweet illusions of Life, . . . so that once more he might not feel himself driven out an infant Ishmael into the desert, with no maternal Hagar to accompany and comfort him.[2]

In *Redburn*, the young man, parting from his mother as he goes off to sea, thinks,

Perhaps she thought me an erring and a wilful boy, and perhaps I was; but if I was, it had been a hardhearted world and hard times that had made me so. I had learned to think much and bitterly before my time. . . . Cold, bitter cold as December, and bleak as its blasts, seemed the world then to me; there is no misanthrope like a boy disappointed; and such was I, with the warm soul of me flogged out by adversity.[3]

Melville's Ishmael mood lasted all his life. In old age, he underscored these lines in a poem by James Thompson:

Pondering a dolorous series of defeats
And black disasters from life's opening day[4]

Melville had what might be called an "Ishmael complex." As with every major complex, it had two sources: personal life experience and identification with an archetypal image. Probably, the major personal cause was the insanity and death of his father and the family's subsequent hardships—most likely experienced unconsciously as a personal rejection by the father. Melville was twelve and a half years old at the time, a striking similarity to the Biblical Ishmael, who was replaced by Isaac at the age of thirteen. In addition, he was rejected by his mother, who favored her first son. From the archetypal standpoint, Melville was in the grip of a figure in the collective psyche. Isaac and Ishmael are only one of many pairs of hostile brothers, one of whom is accepted by God, the other rejected. Cain and Abel, Jacob and Esau, and even Christ and Satan represent the same theme. The opposing brothers embody opposite existential states, acceptance and rejection. As I developed in *Ego and Arche-*

---

[2] Herman Melville, *Pierre* (New York: Grove Press, 1956), p. 125.
[3] *Redburn*, p. 8f.
[4] Arvin, *op. cit.*, p. 12.

type,[5] acceptance and rejection are properly alternating phases in the developmental process. They must be experienced cyclically if one is to reach full maturity. To become identified with only one of these opposites leads to an arrested development. As Esther Harding has pointed out in an unpublished paper, it is the fate of the accepted son to be a sacrificial victim, while it is the fate of the rejected son to be banished to the wilderness. Thus, the one-sided experience of acceptance can be as damaging as rejection.

There are suggestions that the relationship between Melville and his older brother, Gansevoort, was molded by the archetype of the hostile brothers. Herman was the rejected one, Gansevoort the mother's favorite. We have already noted Melville's poem beginning,

> I made the junior feel his place,
> Subserve the senior, love him too.

Gansevoort's life followed a course strangely reciprocal to Herman's. In their youth Gansevoort was the conventionally successful one, opening a law office and later becoming prominent in politics. Herman, on the contrary, was lost and aimless, finally going to sea on a whaler. In 1844, Gansevoort campaigned vigorously for James Polk as president. When Polk was elected, Gansevoort was awarded a post at the American legation in London. Meanwhile, Herman was discovering his own calling as a writer. *Typee* was published in 1846, and that same year, Gansevoort, after helping Herman find a publisher in London, died of an obscure illness at the age of thirty. It seems that Herman's success was Gansevoort's failure. At least, the course of events is compatible with the theory that Herman and Gansevoort were mutually identified with the archetypal pattern of the opposite brothers: as one waxes, the other must wane.

If Melville was personally identified with the figure of Ishmael, what he wrote out of that identification has a more than personal meaning. In our Judeo-Christian culture, Ishmael represents the opposite attitude. To speak as Ishmael means to speak from a position outside the orthodox and conventional. It means the antithesis of collective, conscious values. Ishmael is an anti-Isaac and, by extension, an anti-Christ. Hence, the introduction of his name in the novel's first sentence prepares for the Luciferian contents to follow.

[5] Edward F. Edinger, *Ego and Archetype* (New York: G. P. Putnam's Sons, 1972), p. 37f.

Most of the action is seen through the eyes of Ishmael, the narrator of the tale. He will thus represent the author's ego, the operative conscious attitude, an alienated attitude determined largely by Melville's experiences of rejection. His novel speaks so deeply to us today because this state of alienated meaninglessness is so prevalent in twentieth-century man. In the story of Ishmael's voyage we recognize dimly the state of our own souls.

If there is any doubt that the name Ishmael symbolizes a state of alienation and despair, this doubt cannot survive a reading of the first paragraph:

> Call me Ishmael. Some years ago—never mind how long precisely—having little or no money in my purse, and nothing particular to interest me on shore, I thought I would sail about a little and see the watery part of the world. It is a way I have of driving off the spleen, and regulating the circulation. Whenever I find myself growing grim about the mouth; whenever it is a damp, drizzly November in my soul; whenever I find myself involuntarily pausing before coffin warehouses, and bringing up the rear of every funeral I meet; and especially whenever my hypos get such an upper hand of me, that it requires a strong moral principle to prevent me from deliberately stepping into the street, and methodically knocking people's hats off—then, I account it high time to get to sea as soon as I can. This is my substitute for pistol and ball. With a philosophical flourish Cato throws himself upon his sword; I quietly take to the ship. There is nothing surprising in this. If they but knew it, almost all men in their degree, some time or other, cherish very nearly the same feelings towards the ocean with me.

This mood of a "damp, drizzly November in the soul" is the psychological starting point of the whole drama. It is a state of depression, emptiness, and alienation from life values. Meaning is gone, and without meaning life is intolerable—hence the thoughts of suicide. Today, this state of mind commonly leads a person into psychotherapy. When old values and one's habitual life orientation have been lost, when libido has drained off into the unconscious, an oppressive state of sterility and hopelessness sets in. Odysseus' mood before his *nekyia* is characteristic:

> . . . my spirit was broken within me and I wept as I sat on the bed, nor had my heart any longer desire to live and behold the light of the sun.[6]

[6] *Odyssey*, Book X, lines 496–98.

Since the descent into the unconscious involves a reversal of the usual flow of psychic energy, its initiation requires an urgent psychic need. The opening paragraph of *Moby-Dick* strikes the same note, as do almost all the classic examples of the *nekyia*. Here is Job's description:

> Let the day perish wherein I was born.
> And the night which said
> "A man-child is conceived."
>
> . . .
>
> Why did I not die at birth,
> Come forth from the womb and expire?
> Why did the knees receive me?
> Or why the breasts that I should suck?
> For then I should have lain down
> And been quiet:
> I should have slept. [Job 3]

Dante's *Divine Comedy* begins:

> Midway upon the journey of our life
> I found that I was in a dusky wood;
> For the right path, whence I had strayed, was lost.
> Ah me! How hard a thing it is to tell
> The wildness of that rough and savage place,
> The very thought of which brings back my fear!
> So bitter was it, death is little more so.[7]

And Bunyan's *Pilgrim's Progress* opens:

> I saw a man clothed in rags, standing in a certain place, with his face from his own house, a book in his hand, and a great burden upon his back. I looked, and saw him open the book, and read therein; and as he read, he wept, and trembled; and not being able longer to contain, he broke out with a lamentable cry, saying, "What shall I do?"

We have no dearth of modern descriptions of the alienated psyche. So-called existential literature is full of them. Take, for instance, Eliot's "The Waste Land":

> What are the roots that clutch, What branches grow
> Out of this stony rubbish? Son of man,
> You cannot say, or guess, for you know only

[7] Dante, *The Divine Comedy*, Lawrence Grant White, trans. (New York: Pantheon Books, 1948), p. 1.

A heap of broken images, where the sun beats,
And the dead tree gives no shelter, the cricket no relief,
And the dry stone no sound of water.

Or "The Hollow Men":

This is the dead land
This is the cactus land
Here the stone images
Are raised, here they receive
The supplication of a dead man's hand
Under the twinkle of a fading star.

Job, Dante, Bunyan, and Eliot are all writing out of the archetypal experience of the wilderness, the place of exile, the wilderness of ejected Adam and Eve, of Cain, of Ishmael, and of the temptation of Jesus. It is the psychological state of the barren ego, cut off from the central source of psychic energy, the Self. What makes the image of exile in the wilderness so important today is that it expresses a widespread current state of mind. A patient at the beginning of analysis dreamt, "I have been banished to the cold, barren wastes of Siberia and am wandering about aimlessly." If she were a poet, she could have written another "The Waste Land."

Perhaps the most significant parallel to the opening of *Moby-Dick* is the first scene of Goethe's *Faust*. Faust is contemplating suicide. These scattered lines suggest his mood:

O couldst thou, light of the full moon,
Look now thy last upon my pain,
Thou for whom I have sat belated
So many midnights here and waited.

Oh! Am I still stuck in this jail?
This God-damned dreary hole in the wall.

Cooped up among these heaps of books,
Gnawed by worms, coated with dust,

Infinite nature, where can I tap thy veins?
Where are thy breasts, whose well-springs of all life
On which hang heaven and earth,

Towards which my dry breast strains?
They well up, they give drink, but I fell drought and dearth.[8]

Taken as a whole, *Faust* provides the closest parallel of all to *Moby-Dick*. As will appear later, *Moby-Dick* also involves a pact with the Devil. What Burckhardt said about the German masterpiece is equally true of *Moby-Dick:*

> *Faust* is a genuine myth, i.e., a great primordial image, in which every man has to discover his own being and destiny in his own way. . . . There was an Oedipus chord in every Greek that longed to be directly touched and to vibrate after its own fashion. The same is true of Faust and the German nation.[9]

Moby-Dick could be called the American *Faust*. Ishmael and Ahab are primordial images that lie deep in the American soul. This makes the study of *Moby-Dick*, for an American particularly, much more than an intellectual exercise.

These mythological and literary analogies demonstrate that Melville was writing out of the universal, archetypal theme of the night sea journey, or descent to the underworld. The theme has no national or racial boundaries. It is found everywhere because it refers to an innate, necessary psychic movement which must take place sooner or later when the conscious ego has exhausted the resources and energies of a given life attitude. To find the new attitude and new energies to rejuvenate the sterile, empty conscious state, a descent to the unconscious must be made to contact what Goethe called "infinite nature" whose breasts are the wellsprings of life. While Melville's theme is thus a universal, basically human one, the imagery, the specific content which embodies and gives it concrete realization, is typically American. *Moby-Dick* is the first major product of the American imagination to give authentic expression to the mythological depths of the collective American psyche.

The theme of alienation may also have a particular relevance for the American mind because all Americans are immigrants, or recent descendents of immigrants. The experience of being uprooted from a mother country and transplanted to an alien wilderness is in the

[8] Goethe's *Faust*, Louis MacNeice, trans. (New York: Oxford University Press, Galaxy Books, 1960), p. 20f.
[9] Quoted by Jung in *Symbols of Transformation*, CW 5 (Princeton, N.J.: Princeton University Press, 1956), par. 45, n. 45.

psychic heritage of us all. Most American genealogies go back to dissidents, malcontents, and outcasts, or, alternatively, to the rejected, persecuted, and enslaved. Americans have always fancied that the future was theirs, but the lack of a past is a perennial source of cultural inferiority feelings (which we compensate by technological arrogance). Ishmael and his obverse, Ahab, could well symbolize a major complex in the collective American psyche.

The first paragraph tells us that Ishmael is going to sea to escape a mood of suicidal depression. It is followed by a description of the fascination that water has for everyone.

> . . . meditation and water are wedded forever. . . . Why did the old Persians hold the sea holy? Why did the Greeks give it a separate deity, and own brother of Jove? Surely all this is not without meaning. And still deeper the meaning of that story of Narcissus, who because he could not grasp the tormenting mild image he saw in the fountain, plunged into it and was drowned. [Chapter 1]

The sea is an image of the collective unconscious, the infinite mother nature out of which all life comes. Depending on the conscious attitude with which it is approached, it can be the source of treasures and new life, or it can be the womb of nonbeing that swallows up the weak, regressive ego. Whenever the activated unconscious is being faced, the conscious attitude is of crucial importance. An earnest, responsible attitude is imperative, for to approach the activated unconscious with a passive, escapist intent can be courting psychic suicide. It is the difference between diving into water purposefully or falling into it backward. In light of this distinction, the first paragraph of *Moby-Dick* strikes an ominous note; it clearly shows an element of regressive escapism in Ishmael's taking to sea. Furthermore, the whole tone of the narrative in this opening paragraph is lacking in earnest and serious intent. There is a flippant, half-humorous approach to a matter of the utmost gravity. This careless, almost jocular attitude is sometimes seen in patients beginning psychotherapy. It is a defense against a profound fear of the unconscious and generally indicates a weakness of the ego. The opening sentences tell us that Ishmael's night sea journey is going to be an unusually perilous one.

Another aspect of the first chapter is worth noting: a strong sense of destiny accompanies Ishmael's decision to go to sea.

. . . [that] I should now take it into my head to go on a whaling voyage; this the invisible police officer of the Fates, who had the constant surveillance of me, and secretly dogs me, and influences me in some unaccountable way—he can better answer than any one else. And, doubtless, my going on this whaling voyage, formed part of the grand programme of Providence that was drawn up a long time ago.

This is the first of the many references to fate and providence which saturate the entire book with a powerful sense of destiny. Ahab, in particular, frequently expresses this feeling. A sense of destiny is shared by geniuses and madmen. It is evidence of being in contact with the collective unconscious and of the realization that one's life course is governed largely by transconscious factors. The effects of such a realization may be either creative or pathological depending on the ego's ability to relate responsibly to the experience without inflation.

So Ishmael, following his destiny, sets out to sea,

> the great flood-gates of the wonder-world swung open, and in the wild conceits that swayed me to my purpose, two and two there floated into my inmost soul, endless processions of the whale, and, mid most of them all, one grand hooded phantom, like a snow hill in the air. [Chapter 1]

A passage in *Pierre*, the book Melville wrote after *Moby-Dick*, gives us some idea of the psychological meaning of this voyage in search of the whale. The same phrase, "hooded phantoms," appears just after the hero, Pierre, has suffered a severe shock:

> "Hitherto I have ever held but lightly," thought Pierre, "all stories of ghostly mysticalness in man; my creed of this world leads me to believe . . . only in visible flesh and audible breath." . . . But now . . . he would lose himself in the most surprising and preternatural ponderings, which baffled all the introspective cunning of his mind. Himself was too much for himself. He felt that what he had always before considered the solid land of veritable reality, was now being audaciously encroached upon by bannered armies of hooded phantoms, disembarking in his soul, as from flotillas of spectre-boats.[10]

This passage amplifies the unusual phrase "hooded phantoms" in *Moby-Dick*. It says that the "great flood-gates of the wonder-world"

[10] *Pierre*, Book III, Chapter 2.

open to let in "bannered armies of hooded phantoms, disembarking in his soul." In other words, the collective unconscious has opened, letting in fascinating, disturbing images to challenge Melville's perceptions of ordinary reality. He is aware of an inner, psychic reality as commanding as outer reality. His capacity to assimilate and understand these images is challenged. They threaten his reality adaptation and question his sanity. In short, these parallel passages, together with a vast amount of internal evidence, indicate that the autonomous achetypal psyche was powerfully and dangerously activated during Melville's writing of *Moby-Dick*.

In Ishmael's inner vision, the "endless processions of the whale" occurred "two by two," in pairs. This image testifies to the fact that the activation of the unconscious is usually accompanied by an experience of the pairs of opposites. A major theme of *Moby-Dick* is the problem of the opposites. As we proceed we shall encounter numerous antitheses: alienation and inflation, courage and cowardice, strength and weakness, black and white, good and evil, the bounded land and the boundless sea, height and depth, the universal and the particular, Christian and pagan, primitive and civilized, the outer world and the inner soul, spirit and matter, destiny and free will, love and hate, calm and turbulence, delight and woe, orthodox and heretic, reason and madness, God and man.

4 QUEEQUEG, THE PRIMITIVE SHADOW

IN CHAPTER TWO, "The Carpet-Bag," Ishmael sets out for New Bedford, and the journey into the unconscious begins. What Melville means by the carpet-bag is revealed in a letter to Hawthorne in which he writes,

> For all men who say *yes*, lie; and all men who say *no*—why, they are in the happy condition of judicious unincumbered travellers in Europe; they cross the frontiers into Eternity with nothing but a carpet-bag— that is to say, the Ego.[1]

Upon arrival in New Bedford, he is immediately confronted with

[1] Leyda, *op. cit.*, p. 410.

images of darkness and death. It is a Saturday night in December, the darkest month of the year, when the sun itself seems threatened by death, "a very dark and dismal night, bitingly cold and cheerless. . . . Such dreary streets! blocks of blackness, not houses, and here and there a candle, like a candle moving about in a tomb." He stumbles by mistake into a Negro church, like

> the black parliament sitting in Tophet . . . and the preacher's text was about the blackness of darkness, and the weeping and wailing and teeth-gnashing there.

Tophet was a valley south of Jerusalem where children were offered as burnt sacrifices to Molech. Later it became a dumping ground for dead bodies and filth of all kinds. A perpetual fire was kept burning there, hence it became a symbol for hell. This image indicates that Ishmael felt himself descending, like Dante, into Hell—the unconscious region of fiery, torturing, repressed passion and desire. Finally, coming to the Spouter Inn, where he decides to stay, Ishmael continues in his dark mood, having ominous reflections about the proprietor's name, Peter Coffin.

This emphasis on blackness and death, characteristic of the early phase of the descent into the unconscious, corresponds to the first phase of the alchemical transformation process, called the *nigredo*, or blackening. Concerning this phase, Jung says,

> There have always been people who, not satisfied with the dominants of conscious life, set forth—under cover and by devious routes, to their destruction or salvation—to seek direct experience of the eternal roots, and, following the lure of the restless, unconscious psyche, found themselves in the wilderness where, like Jesus, they come up against the son of darkness. Thus an old alchemist prays. "Purge the horrible darkness of our mind." The author of this sentence must have been undergoing the experience of *nigredo*, the first stage of the work, which was felt as melancholia in alchemy and corresponds to the encounter with the shadow in psychology.[2]

Further images of chaos, death, and destruction greet us at the beginning of chapter three. Ishmael enters the Spouter Inn and is immediately confronted with a shadowy, ominous, enigmatic painting

---

[2] *Psychology and Alchemy*, CW 12 (Princeton, N.J.: Princeton University Press, 1953), par. 41.

on the wall. This painting reflects Ishmael's own inner darkness into which he is gazing. It functions as a kind of Rorschach ink blot to evoke the unconscious images that are preoccupying him. He asks himself what it is. It is "chaos bewitched," or perhaps

the Black Sea in a midnight gale.—It is the unnatural combat of the four primal elements.—It is a Hyperborean winter scene.—It is the breaking up of the ice-bound streams of time.

Finally he decides.

The picture represents a Cape-Horner in a great hurricane; the half-foundered ship weltering there with its three dismantled masts alone visible; and an exasperated whale, purposing to spring clean over the craft, is in the enormous act of impaling himself upon the three mast-heads.

This image presages the outcome of the voyage he is about to start.

Ishmael seeks lodging and learns that he must share a bed with a savage harpooner, Queequeg. Thus the darkness which was initially diffuse and shapeless takes on form, personified as Queequeg, the primitive shadow figure. The shadow is the first personification to be met in an analysis of the unconscious. It is the antithesis of the conscious personality, embodying those characteristics, potentialities, and attitudes that have been rejected or depreciated by the ego. Furthermore, since there is no differentiation between contents in the unconscious, everything merging with everything else, the shadow on initial meeting carries the impact of the unconscious as a whole. Only after its encounter with the conscious ego does it begin to separate from other aspects of the unconscious and lose the feature of totality.

Queequeg is described in chapters three, four, ten, eleven, and twelve. Ishmael first meets the savage harpooner in chapter three and is frightened by his alien appearance, his strangely tattooed skin, and his pagan religious ritual. He is the very opposite of Ishmael's civilized, Christian consciousness. Characteristically, Ishmael expects to be attacked by Queequeg. The ego usually assumes the shadow has a hostile intent. This is a projection. The ego feels hostile toward the shadow and expects hostility in return, which, under the circumstances, is quite likely. As a rule the unconscious shows the ego the same face that the ego shows to it. Ishmael quickly comes to this realization:

What is all this fuss I have been making about, thought I to myself—the man's a human being just as I am; he has just as much reason to fear me, as I have to be afraid of him. [Chapter 3]

After sharing Queequeg's bed for the night, Ishmael awakens next morning in the heavy embrace of the dark man's arm, "this arm of his tattooed all over with an interminable Cretan labyrinth of a figure." [Chapter 4] Later in the book, this same association with the labyrinth of the Minotaur in the myth of Theseus appears in a description of the whale, "supplied with a remarkable involved Cretan labyrinth of vermicilli-like vessels." [Chapter 85] Again, in *Pierre*, the labyrinth image is applied to Isabel, the dark anima figure, infatuation with whom leads Pierre into the unconscious, "like Cretan labyrinths, to which thy life's cord is leading thee."[3]

The labyrinth or maze is a symbol of the unconscious, particularly its dangerous aspect, which threatens confusion and disorientation. Theseus could dare to enter it only with the helpful orientation of Ariadne's thread. Ariadne is an anima figure; her thread signifies a connecting link between the ego (Theseus) and the anima, or feeling life. In the Cretan labyrinth lived a masculine monster, the minotaur, representing primitive, undifferentiated male instinctuality. The myth suggests that one may dare to confront his unregenerate lust and power urge only if he can hold to the guiding thread of human feeling-relatedness, which gives him orientation and prevents his dismemberment and dissolution in the chaos of instinctive drives. If Queequeg is a labyrinth, he is also an Ariadne. As we shall see shortly, he evokes in Ishmael a capacity for love and human feeling which will redeem him and ultimately save him from the catastrophe of the Pequod's voyage.

So Queequeg, the primitive, is Ishmael's shadow, but he is more than a personal shadow; his roots go deep. He is a piece of primeval nature itself, a personification of the original whole man at home with nature and himself. A close, indeed inseparable, relationship quickly develops between Ishmael and Queequeg. This is the theme of the primitive brother or friend, the hero's necessary counterpart who provides him with a certain completeness. For instance, in the Epic of Gilgamesh, the dark primitive counterpart is Enkidu, who helps the hero to face and overcome the cosmic bull.

[3] *Pierre*, Book X, Chapter 1.

The wholeness Queequeg embodies is alluded to by the fact that he has black squares tattooed on his body and that his mark is the Maltese cross. Many other descriptive passages about Queequeg indicate this wholeness. He had a "certain lofty bearing" and "looked like a man who had never cringed and never had a creditor." In a fine passage, his self-possession is described:

> Savages are strange beings; at times you do not know exactly how to take them. At first they are overawing; their calm self-collectedness of simplicity seems a Socratic wisdom. I had noticed also that Queequeg never consorted at all, or but very little, with the other seamen in the inn. He made no advances whatever; appeared to have no desire to enlarge the circle of his acquaintants. All this struck me as mighty singular; yet, upon second thoughts, there was something almost sublime in it. Here was a man some twenty thousand miles from home, by the way of Cape Horn, that is—which was the only way he could get there—thrown among people as strange to him as though he were in the planet Jupiter; and yet he seemed entirely at his ease; preserving the utmost serenity; content with his own companionship; always equal to himself. [Chapter 10]

Natural dignity and equanimity are the consequences of being related to the original totality of the psyche. Further evidence of the wholeness which Queequeg conveys is provided by the healing effect he has on Ishmael. "Whole" and "heal" are cognate words—to heal means to make whole. This is the effect Ishmael experiences. He says,

> I began to be sensible of strange feelings. I felt a melting in me. No more my splintered heart and maddened hand were turned against the wolfish world. This soothing savage had redeemed it. [Chapter 10]

Ishmael has been redeemed from his initial state of alienation by his encounter with Queequeg, who is a composite of shadow and Self. The "melting" within him indicates that a reconnection with the Self is accompanied by an awakened capacity to love. Ishmael's healing is only a partial process, however; Ahab's greater alienation is yet to come.

The information Melville gives about Queequeg's life is significant. He was the native of a primitive island, the son of its king, and had a desperate urgency to visit civilization. He stole aboard a visiting whaleship and throwing himself full length upon the deck, grappled a ring-bolt there, and swore not to let it go, though hacked to pieces.

In vain the captain threatened to throw him overboard; suspended a cutlass over his naked wrists; Queequeg was the son of a King, and Queequeg budged not. Struck by his desperate dauntlessness, and his wild desire to visit Christendom, the captain at last relented, and told him he might make himself at home. [Chapter 12]

His urgent need to make contact with civilization is important. It represents the striving of the shadow for consciousness. Queequeg's heroic efforts to go to sea and learn about the white man's civilization is a movement in the unconscious reciprocal to the depressive escapism which sent Ishmael to sea. It is as though ego and shadow were running toward each other from their opposite positions. Ishmael leaves his sterile life on land, Queequeg leaves his primitive, unconscious island paradise, each in search of the other.

The shadow's striving for admission to consciousness is a common theme in psychotherapy. It is often represented in dreams by primitive or uncouth men who are attempting to break into a house. Such dreams, like Queequeg's urge to visit civilization, indicate the shadow's urge to participate and realize itself in consciousness. The shadow carries aspects of the personality rejected by the ego because they do not fit its ideal image. The shadow is thus branded as inferior and unacceptable. At a certain point in development, psychological growth cannot proceed until this attitude is changed and the shadow is welcomed into consciousness. Queequeg must leave his unconscious paradise isle and be accepted at the civilized or conscious level if the capacities he represents are to be realized in actual life.

It is by no means easy to accept the shadow. It usually involves facing one's most serious weaknesses and inferiorities. It is commonly thought that the acceptance of a weakness gives it a reality it will not have otherwise. The ego operates on the false assumption that it can decide what aspects of the psyche may be permitted existence. Acceptance of a weakness is equated with the condoning of it; that is, the ego acts as a judge which approves or condemns various aspects of the personality. This is the repressive attitude which split the original wholeness of the psyche and created the shadow in the first place. However, for the adult, the psyche in all its aspects is a given, a priori fact. Since it exists and has its effects, whether consciously accepted or not, it is greatly to the individual's advantage to be conscious rather than unconscious of his own reality.

After Ishmael gets over his initial horror at the prospect of sleeping with a savage, he sees Queequeg chiefly in positive terms. This is commonly the effect of facing the shadow; it turns positive, at least in part. In addition, Ishmael represents an ego which is acutely aware of its own inadequacies. In such a case, much of the potential strength of the personality sinks into the unconscious, where it is carried by the shadow, making this figure more positive. We then speak of a positive shadow. Queequeg is such a positive shadow, carrying major strength and assets as yet unrealized by consciousness. His positive character is particularly evident in the prominent, masculine attributes he embodies. In contrast to Ishmael, who is moody, depressive, and subject to regressive tendencies, Queequeg is full of strength, dignity, and purposefulness, a harpooner who has his harpoon with him constantly. "That barbed iron was in lieu of a scepter now." The harpoon, a variant of the spear, belongs to the whole body of masculine libido symbols—sword, arrow, ray, phallus, staff, light, etc. These images all refer to the masculine principle which, on the instinctive level, is manifested by aggressive, self-asserting power and, on the psychological level, by initiative, disciplined purposefulness, penetrating, discriminating rationality, and the clarifying, creative power of Logos. The figure of Queequeg carries these capacities in a primitive, undifferentiated form.

The relation between Ishmael and Queequeg reveals a weakness in Melville's personality, namely, that his masculine psychic functions were still largely unconscious. Several commentators on Melville have noted a latent homosexual predisposition in the almost erotic description of Ishmael and Queequeg as a cozy, loving pair, almost a married couple. In other of Melville's writings also we find intense, emotional relationships between men. I doubt that there is any question of overt homosexuality here. Certain circumstances tend to evoke intense, emotional relationships when men without women are grouped together, subject to mutual tasks or mutual dangers, such as at sea or in the army. Such friendships generally signify a need to bolster or consolidate a weak connection to the masculine principle. Where relationship with the father has been inadequate, the unconscious, unrealized masculinity is projected onto the friend, and union with him is expected to restore the missing psychic content. These considerations are pertinent to Melville's psychology. We need only recall his intense response to Hawthorne. That Melville was cut off from a full masculine functioning of discriminating rationality is evident in the following remarks from a letter he wrote to Hawthorne:

> I stand for the heart. To the dogs with the head! I had rather be a fool with a heart, than Jupiter Olympus with his head. The reason the mass of men fear God, and at bottom dislike Him, is because they rather distrust His heart and fancy Him all brain like a watch.[4]

Here Melville is giving conscious allegiance to the Dionysian aspect of life and depreciating its balancing opposite, the Apollonian. The discriminating, structuring, clarifying function of the masculine principle is weak. This is Melville's defect. It accounts for a certain wild unpredictability in his writings, which can fluctuate between imaginative brilliance and banal sentimentality. Queequeg's harpoon symbolizes this missing rationality.

But Queequeg is more than a figure in Melville's individual psychology. He is the collective shadow of nineteenth-century man, an aspect of the collective psyche which is only now, one hundred years later, beginning to emerge into consciousness. Queequeg, the natural, pagan, primitive man whose culture and psychic integrity were destroyed by self-righteous Christian missionaries (about whom Melville makes some caustic remarks in his early books), is the shadow and adversary of the nineteenth-century collective canon of religious orthodoxy. Ishmael confronts this fact when he is asked to share Queequeg's idolatrous religious ceremony. He contemplates this question in the following passage:

> I was a good Christian born and bred in the bosom of the infallible Presbyterian Church. How then could I unite with this idolator in worshipping his piece of wood? But what is worship? thought I. Do you suppose, Ishmael, that the magnanimous God of heaven and earth—pagans and all included—can possibly be jealous of an insignificant bit of black wood? Impossible! But what is worship?—to do the will of God—*that* is worship. And what is the will of God?—to do to my fellow man what I would have my fellow man to do to me—*that* is the will of God. Now, Queequeg is my fellow man. And what do I wish that this Queequeg would do to me? Why, to unite with me in my particular Presbyterian form of worship. Consequently, I must

4 Metcalf, *op. cit.*, p. 109.

then unite with him in his, ergo, I must turn idolator. So I kindled the shavings; helped prop up the innocent little idol; offered him burnt biscuit with Queequeg; salaamed before him twice or thrice; kissed his nose; and that done, we undressed and went to bed, at peace with our own consciences, and all the world. [Chapter 10]

Ishmael's respect of Queequeg's primitive piety would be anathema to orthodox nineteenth-century Christendom. It admits that the Christian myth is not the unique, superlative, and final one. For twentieth-century man, who is rapidly losing all sense of transpersonal meaning, Christian or otherwise, this admission is not a problem. In fact, the breaking up of the dominant collective myth is causing modern man to search the depths of the primitive psyche for the source of the lost religious attitude. Nevertheless, Ishmael turns pagan with suspicious speed. With astonishing ease, he turns his back on the whole Judeo-Christian heritage, and, following his own individual reasoning, which runs counter to centuries of tradition, he turns idolator. At this point the door is opened for Ahab, another idolator. All the fateful events he brings in his train are the inevitable consequences of this initial act. We are reminded of the careless, flippant attitude with which Ishmael decided to go to sea. Here is the man who could say, "I stand for the heart. To the dogs with head!" This is no responsible dialogue with the unconscious but rather a capitulation to it. It is another omen that the coming voyage will be a dangerous one.

That Ishmael's meeting with Queequeg is to have fateful, overpowering consequences is indicated by a childhood recollection which Ishmael associates with Queequeg. Following the first night they sleep together, Ishmael awakes to find Queequeg hugging him, and the strange sensations this evokes recall a childhood experience:

When I was a child, I well remember a somewhat similar circumstance that befell me; whether it was a reality or a dream, I never could entirely settle. The circumstance was this. I had been cutting up some caper or other—I think it was trying to crawl up the chimney, as I had seen a little sweep do a few days previously; and my stepmother who, somehow or other, was all the time whipping me, or sending me to bed supperless,—my mother dragged me by the legs out of the chimney and packed me off to bed, though it was only two o'clock in the afternoon of the 21st of June, the longest day in the year in our hemisphere. I felt dreadfully. But there was no help for it, so upstairs I went to my little room in the third floor, undressed myself as slowly as possible so as to kill time, and with a bitter sigh got between the sheets.

I lay there dismally calculating that sixteen hours must elapse before I could hope for a resurrection. Sixteen hours in bed! The small of my back ached to think of it. And it was so light too; the sun was shining in at the window, and a great rattling of coaches in the streets, and the sound of gay voices all over the house. I felt worse and worse —at last I got up, dressed, and softly going down in my stockinged feet, sought out my stepmother, and suddenly threw myself at her feet, beseeching her as a particular favor to give me a good slippering for my misbehavior; anything indeed but condemning me to lie abed such an unendurable length of time. But she was the best and most conscientious of stepmothers, and back I had to go to my room. For several hours I lay there broad awake, feeling a great deal worse than I have ever done since, even from the greatest subsequent misfortunes. At last I must have fallen into a troubled nightmare of a doze; and slowly waking from it—half-steeped in dreams—I opened my eyes, and the before sun-lit room was now wrapped in outer darkness. Instantly I felt a shock running through all my frame; nothing was to be seen, and nothing was to be heard; but a supernatural hand seemed placed in mine. My arm hung over the counterpane, and the nameless, unimaginable, silent form or phantom, to which the hand belonged, seemed closely seated by my bedside. For what seemed ages piled on ages, I lay there frozen with the most awful fears, not daring to drag my hand away; yet ever thinking that if I could but stir it one single inch, the horrid spell would be broken. I knew not how this consciousness at last glided away from me; but waking in the morning, I shudderingly remembered it all, and for days and weeks and months afterwards I lost myself in confounding attempts to explain the mystery. [Chapter 4]

This memory rings true and surely corresponds, at least approximately, to an actual happening. It refers to an experience of the objective psyche—that level of psyche which is autonomous and independent of conscious control—such as have always been described as encounters with deity. Rudolf Otto in his excellent book, *The Idea of the Holy*, writing of the *mysterium tremendum* in religious experience, uses the adjective "numinous" to describe such encounters.[5] An experience is numinous when it carries an excess of meaning or

[5] Rudolf Otto, *The Idea of the Holy* (New York: Oxford University Press, 1950).

energy, transcending the capacity of the conscious personality to encompass or understand it. The individual is awed, overwhelmed, and yet fascinated. The scriptures of all religions describe the numinous in their records of the encounter with God, or the divine prophetic inspiration. These all refer to experiences of the objective psyche, always experienced as something "wholly other," possessing indisputable authority. Such an experience was that of Moses and the burning bush and the vision of Paul on the road to Damascus.

The touch of the celestial hand brings to mind a similar image in a vision of Daniel. In Daniel 10:10 we read, "And behold, a hand touched me and set me trembling on my hands and knees." Other prophets used the same image to describe the coming of visions or revelations saying, "the hand of the Lord was upon me" [Ezek. 37:1, Kings 8:46, Rev. 1:17, etc.]

The experience of a small boy who has been punished harshly and imagines that a presence is sitting on his bed, holding his hand, carried potentially some sense of comfort and reassurance. Although Melville did not experience it that way according to his description, the happening itself seems to say, "Never mind your mean stepmother who does not understand you. I am your destiny and I am with you. Take your comfort from me." A sense of destiny can be felt as an intolerable burden or as a source of deep-seated security. Jung describes the latter feeling in his autobiography:

> From the beginning I had a sense of destiny, as though my life was assigned to me by fate and had to be fulfilled. This gave me an inner security. . . . Nobody could rob me of the conviction that it was enjoined upon me to do what God wanted and not what I wanted. That gave me the strength to go my own way.[6]

In *Mardi*, Melville uses the image of the divine hand to describe the power not his own that compels him to write:

> My cheek blanches white while I write; I start at the scratch of my pen; my own mad brood of eagles devour me; fain I could unsay this audacity; but an iron-mailed hand clenches mine in a vice, and prints down every letter in my spite. Fain would I hurl off this Dionysius that rides me; my thoughts crush me down till I groan; in far fields I hear the song of the reaper, while I slave and faint in this cell. The

[6] C. G. Jung, *Memories, Dreams, Reflections* (New York: Pantheon Books, 1963), p. 48.

fever runs through me like lava; my hot brain burns like a coal; and like many a monarch, I am less to be envied, than the veriest hind in the land. [Chapter 119]

This passage leaves no doubt that the grip of the divine hand was Melville's creative vocation, which possessed him against his conscious will. The source of his creative inspiration is indifferent to his personal choice or welfare. The numinous power of transpersonal energies can have destructive, crippling effects on the ego; witness Job's exclamation, "Have pity on me, have pity on me, O you my friends, for the hand of God has touched me!" [Job 19:21]. Both the creative and destructive aspects of the "touch of God" are evident in Melville's life and work, as shall become increasingly apparent as we proceed. When he visited the Holy Land in 1857, he was overwhelmed by its sense of bleak, stony desolation. He wrote in his journal, "Is the desolation of the land the result of the fatal embrace of the Deity? Hapless are the favorites of heaven."[7] From an early age, he had evidently experienced "the embrace of the Deity." It gave him a profound sense of personal destiny, as revealed in a remark to his publisher, written in 1849, two years before *Moby-Dick:*

> . . . we that write and print have all our books predestinated—and for me, I shall write such things as the Great Publisher of Mankind ordained ages before he published "The World" . . .[8]

The "embrace of the Deity" gave him creative contact with the collective unconscious and its vast store of primordial images, enriching his expressive powers to their maximum in *Moby-Dick*. He felt himself "like a frigate . . . full with a thousand souls . . . my memory is a life beyond birth . . . with all the past and present pouring in me, I roll down my billow from afar." [*Mardi*, Chapter 119] However, just as a slender wire can carry briefly an overcharge of electricity providing a moment of intense illumination before being consumed by the overload, so Melville's conscious personality served briefly as a conductor of brilliant archetypal energies. But their voltage was too great for the conducting substance. The intense illumination of *Moby-Dick* was to require a long period of convalescence and repair.

[7] Herman Melville, from "Introduction" by Walter Bezanson, *Clarel* (New York: Hendricks House, 1960), p. xx.
[8] Metcalf, *op. cit.*, p. 71.

5 THE SIGN OF JONAH

IN THE INTERLUDE following his meeting with Queequeg and prior to his signing on the ship, Ishmael attends the whalemen's chapel and hears a dramatic sermon on Jonah. This sermon presents us with the voyage of Jonah as an analogy to the coming voyage of Ishmael. We must therefore consider the psychological meaning of the Jonah story as well as the general archetypal motif of which it is a particular example. Basically, the widespread mythological theme of the hero devoured by a monster goes like this:

> A hero is devoured by a water-monster in the West. The animal travels with him (inside) to the East. Meanwhile, the hero lights a fire in the belly of the monster, and feeling hungry, cuts himself a piece of the heart. Soon afterwards, he notices that the fish has glided onto dry land; he immediately begins to cut open the animal from within; then he slips out. It was so hot in the fish's belly that all his hair has fallen out. The hero may at the same time free all those who were previously devoured by the monster.[1]

This myth depicts the archetypal theme of heroic incest—a purposeful descent into the maternal womb, the depths of the unconscious, for the purpose of transformation and rebirth. The monster represents unconscious psychic energy in its natural, elemental, and undifferentiated state. It is untamed animal energy, not yet available for conscious civilized functioning. The ego is in constant danger of being devoured by the monster, that is, of being possessed by raw unredeemed instinctuality. This danger is symbolized by the image of incest with the mother, but in the vast majority of cases has nothing to do with actual desire for intercourse. The notion that it does stems from the Freudian fallacy of taking psychic images concretely rather than symbolically.

If the ego is particularly weak, the threat can be one of psychosis. I recall a patient who suffered periodic catatonic schizophrenia. During a period of remission, he had the following dream: *A huge whale*

---

[1] L. Frobenius, *Das Zeitalter des Sonnengottes*. Cited by Jung, *Symbols of Transformation*, par. 310.

is approaching him. He knows he is going to be swallowed by the whale and that there is nothing he can do to avoid it. He is helplessly awaiting his fate as he awakes. A few days after this dream, he had a relapse of his schizophrenia and lost all contact with reality. This is the meaning, when the conscious personality is weak and regressive, of being swallowed by the monster. When the ego approaches the monster in a purposeful way, with a more heroic attitude, the outcome is different. Another patient, with a much different prognosis, had this dream: *He sees a beautiful, seductive woman on a couch. She is naked and asks him to have intercourse with her. As he approaches, she turns into a horrible, vulturelike monster whose genitals become a devouring mouth. The monster's mouth opens and begins to eat the dreamer's head. Instead of trying to fight his way out of her clutches, he hurries the process by literally crawling down her throat. Once inside, he starts hitting her from within and can hear her cries of pain. He then crawls right out of her in some awful birth process. From her entrails, he rescues a tiny white figure—a wee, gnomelike baby that begins growing as soon as it is released. It turns into a beautiful child, glowing and luminous, evoking an intense feeling of joy and exhilaration.*

This is a remarkable modern parallel to the ancient myths of the hero's purposeful descent into the monster. The beautiful glowing child symbolizes the emergent Self, the central transpersonal value of the psyche, corresponding to the archetype of the *puer æternus*[2] and to the *homunculus* of the alchemists. The dream parallels a Gnostic monster myth which describes the descent of Hibil, the savior-god, into the underworld. Hibil speaks:

> Karkum the great flesh-mountain said unto me: Go, or I shall devour thee. When he spoke thus to me, I was in a casing of swords, sabres, lances, knives, and blades, and I said unto him: Devour me. Then . . . he swallowed me half-way: then he spewed me forth. . . . He spewed venom out of his mouth, for his bowels, his liver, and his reins were cut to pieces.[3]

The casing of knives and blades symbolizes the sharp, discriminating

[2] C. G. Jung, "The Psychology of the Child Archetype," *The Archetypes and the Collective Unconscious*, CW 9, i (Princeton, N.J.: Princeton University Press, 1969), par. 259ff.

[3] Hans Jonas, *The Gnostic Religion* (Boston: Beacon Press, 1958), p. 121.

powers of consciousness, which can break up and dismember the unconscious monster, making its energy available to consciousness. Light is a kind of poison to darkness; consciousness by descending into the unconscious can transform it from within. This can happen, however, only when the conscious attitude is a heroic one and the ego descends into the unconscious purposefully. When it happens to a passive, regressive ego, there is apt to be the opposite effect: the light is poisoned by the darkness.

Jonah was such a reluctant hero, one who attempted to evade the call to psychological development.[4]

> Now the word of the Lord came to Jonah the son of Amittai, saying "Arise, go to Nineveh, that great city, and cry against it; for their wickedness has come up before me." But Jonah rose to flee to Tarshish from the presence of the Lord. [Jonah 1:1–3]

The word of the Lord is an inner imperative, a call from the Self to fulfill one's vocation. But, just as Ishmael's motive was escape, and probably Melville's when he signed on a whaling ship, so Jonah attempts to escape his calling by a regressive sea journey. To be a fugitive from God means psychologically that one is attempting to avoid the demands of his own development and destiny. Such demands stem from the Self—the non-ego center of the psyche—and carry a transcendent or Godlike imperative. When crucial inner development is involved, there can be no freedom of choice; one must choose the necessary and inevitable; failure to so choose amounts to a regression, with perhaps fatal psychic consequences.

When the ego denies an unconscious imperative, the unconscious (God) becomes an avenging pursuer. The Erinys of Greek mythology represent an instance of this psychological fact. Francis Thompson's "The Hound of Heaven" also gives a vivid description of the phenomenon:

> I fled Him, down the nights and down the days;
> I fled Him, down the arches of the years;
> I fled Him, down the labyrinthine ways
> Of my own mind; and in the midst of tears
> I hid from Him, and under running laughter.
> Up vistaed hopes I sped;

[4] See account of Jonah in M. Esther Harding, *Psychic Energy: Its Source and Transformation* (Princeton: Princeton University Press, 1973), pp. 277–302.

And shot, precipitated,
Adown Titanic glooms of chasmed fears,
From those strong Feet that followed, followed after.
But with unhurrying chase,
And unperturbéd pace,
Deliberate speed, majestic instancy,
They beat—and a Voice beat
More instant than the Feet—
All things betray thee, who betrayest Me.

Thompson apparently had good reason to write about being a fugitive from God, if we take his true vocation to have been poetry. For he fled from it for many years, dutifully trying to become a doctor, as his father wished, prevented only by repeated failure to pass his final examinations. He had to leave home and endure the extremes of poverty and distress before he finally could accept himself and his vocation. Concerning the psychological meaning of vocation, Jung writes:

> What is it, in the end, that induces a man to go his own way and to rise out of unconscious identity with the mass as out of a swathing mist? . . . It is what is commonly called *vocation:* an irrational factor that destines a man to emancipate himself from the herd and from its well-worn paths. True personality is always a vocation and puts its trust in it as in God . . . vocation acts like a law of God from which there is no escape. . . . Anyone with a vocation hears the voice of the inner man: he is *called*.[5]

> Only the man who can consciously assent to the power of the inner voice becomes a personality.[6]
>
> . . .
>
> To the extent that a man is untrue to the law of his being and does not rise to personality, he has failed to realize his life's meaning. Fortunately, in her kindness and patience, Nature never puts the fatal question as to the meaning of their lives into the mouths of most people, and where no one asks, no one need answer.[7]

The Jonah myth is a story of vocation refused. Rejecting the call, Jonah encounters Yahweh in the negative aspect of a pursuing and

---

[5] *The Development of Personality,* CW 17 (Princeton, N.J.: Princeton University Press, 1954), par. 299ff.

[6] Ibid., par. 308.

[7] Ibid., par. 314.

devouring whale. "And the Lord appointed a great fish to swallow up Jonah; and Jonah was in the belly of the fish three days and three nights." [Jonah 1:17]

Jonah's sojourn in the whale's belly has both regressive and progressive qualities. The regressive is emphasized in a Jewish legend reported by Ginzberg, according to which Jonah was very comfortable in the belly of the whale, "as comfortable inside of him as in a spacious synagogue." Since Jonah had no incentive to leave, God was obliged to transfer him into a second, smaller fish, where, in cramped distress, he then repented and prayed for deliverance. The same legend sees the progressive side of Jonah's experience. It states:

> The fish carried Jonah whithersoever there was a sight to be seen. He showed him the river from which the ocean flows, showed him the spot at which the Israelites crossed the Red Sea, showed him Gehenna and Sheol, and many other mysteries and wonderful places.[8]

In other words, his confinement was also an initiation into the mysteries of the world. According to Paracelsus too, Jonah saw "mighty mysteries" in the belly of the whale.[9]

Jonah's attempted flight from God means that he did not realize he was dealing with a real deity, a true transpersonal power which cannot be escaped. In other words, he was unconscious; he had not yet experienced the imperious reality of God—the objective psyche. Only in the belly of the whale did he discover that he was indeed dealing wtih a power which transcends the ego and exists separate from it. This is the psychological meaning of being initiated into the mysteries. Such a discovery is a transformative and decisive step in psychic development. It gives us a hint that the same transformative potentialities may exist for Ishmael, who, like Jonah, is a fugitive from God.

So the chief lesson of Father Mapple's sermon is that one destined to be a prophet cannot avoid his ordained mission "to preach the Truth to the face of Falsehood." Melville apparently had a "Jonah reaction" to being gripped by the hand of God. Summoned to be an artist-prophet, to "preach the Truth," yet appalled at the hostility he

---

[8] L. Ginzberg, *Legends of the Bible* (New York: Simon and Schuster, 1956), p. 605.

[9] *Liber Azoth* cited by Jung, *Symbols of Transformation*, par. 509.

should raise and mindful of material necessities, he was in an understandable conflict. He wrote to Hawthorne:

> Truth is the silliest thing under the sun. Try to get a living by the Truth—and go to the soup societies. Let any clergyman try to preach the Truth from its very stronghold, the pulpit, and they would ride him out of his church on his own pulpit bannister. . . . Dollars damn me. . . . What I feel most moved to write, that is banned,—it will not pay. Yet, altogether, write the other way I cannot. So the product is a final hash, and all my books are botches.[10]

Evidently Melville experienced the same divided state as Faust, who exclaims:

> "Two souls alas! are dwelling in my breast;
> And each is fain to leave its brother.
> The one, fast clinging, to the world adheres
> With clutching organs, in love's sturdy lust;
> The other strongly lifts itself from dust
> To yonder high, ancestral spheres."[11]

Jung has described undergoing something of the same conflict in his own early years. He was aware of two personalities within him, which he called No. 1 and No. 2. No. 1 was the empirical, individual ego which relates to commonplace reality—the acquiring of money, reputation, and a realistic life adaptation. Personality No. 2 was completely different. It was a "total vision of life." In No. 2, "light reigned, as in the spacious halls of a royal palace. . . . Here was meaning and historical continuity."[12] In Melville's words, here was awareness that he was "full with a thousand souls," with memory of "a life beyond birth." It is the problem of reconciling the practical requirements of life with one's infinite, eternal soul. To be totally preoccupied with the former is to live a shallow, meaningless life; to be immersed only in the infinite meanings of the collective unconscious is to remain unborn to the world of temporal reality.

Jonah was called by Yahweh to convey the message of God to the city of Nineveh—psychologically, the task of relating the transper-

---

[10] Metcalf, *op. cit.*, p. 108.

[11] Goethe's *Faust*, G. M. Priest, trans. (New York: Knopf, 1963), Part I, Scene 2, ll. 1112-17.

[12] C. G. Jung, *Memories, Dreams, Reflections*, p. 87f.

sonal world (Yahweh) to the conscious, personal, temporal world (Nineveh). It is a task of uniting opposites. As long as one feels he must choose either one or the other, he is caught in an ambivalent conflict, in which all his efforts will be—as Melville called his books—"botches." Jonah swings between identification with first one side, then the other. At first he is identified with the personal, conscious world of the ego and does not want to admit into it the imperative of the transpersonal psyche, God's call. Later, after the people of Nineveh have repented, the king has put on sackcloth and ashes, and Yahweh has spared the city the punishment he threatened, Jonah becomes angry. He has become identified with the transpersonal and has forgotten the temporal. He so relished his role as an assistant to the avenging deity that he is disappointed when punishment is no longer necessary.

6 THE NEKYIA BEGINS

QUEEQUEG's oracular idol, Yojo, has informed him that the selection of a ship must be made by Ishmael entirely without help. In this crucial matter, the ego is obliged to make a conscious and responsible choice. Ishmael chooses the whaleship Pequod. The ship's name derives from the Pequot Indians, the strongest tribe in Massachusetts during the early years of the Puritan settlers. It means destroyer, a fitting name for the ship seeking to kill Moby-Dick. (It is interesting to note that Perseus, with whom whale hunters were later associated, also means destroyer.) The Puritans treated the Pequot Indians with the utmost brutality, declaring war without provocation and massacring them at every opportunity. In June 1637, the English, with Indian allies,

> made a stealthy night attack on a stockaded Pequot town near the Mystic River in Connecticut, burned the town and slaughtered its 600 inhabitants. Wrote the Plymouth governor: 'It was a fearful sight to see them frying in the fire . . . and horrible was the stink and stench thereof. But the victory seemed a sweet sacrifice and they gave praise to God.'[1]

[1] William Brandon, ed., *The American Heritage Book of Indians* (New York: Simon and Schuster, 1961), p. 172.

These are the connotations of the ship named Pequod, a ship heavily freighted with primitive man's bitter vengeance against the brutalities of Christian consciousness.

The Pequod's two chief owners are Captain Peleg and Captain Bildad. The Biblical Peleg was a descendant of Noah's son Shem. His name means division, called thus because he lived when the earth was divided into various linguistic groups, the time of the tower of Babel [Gen. 10:25, 1 Chron. 1:19]. Bildad was one of Job's three friends; his name means son of contention. The owners of the ship thus carry allusions to the tower of Babel and the ordeal of Job. In Melville's novel, Bildad and Peleg are in conflict with one another. Bildad, a self-righteous, Bible-reading man, was prepared to cheat Ishmael of his fair wages on the hypocritical pretense that "Where your treasure is, there will your heart be, also." As a sea captain, he had been a cruel taskmaster whose supposed religious convictions had not softened his treatment of his fellow men. Peleg, on the contrary, is uninterested in orthodox religion. He "cared not a rush for what are called serious things, and indeed deemed those selfsame serious things the veriest of all trifles." Peleg, however, has a conscience. He attempts to treat others fairly, and it is he who insists that Ishmael receive fair wages. This association of cruelty and evil with rigid, orthodox Christianity and of natural kindness with the non-Christian is a recurrent theme in Melville. He saw clearly the black shadow behind the self-righteous Christian orthodoxy of his time. That the owners of the Pequod are a cruel Christian and a kind non-Christian reiterates a basic theme of the voyage to come.

As Ishmael is signing on the Pequod, his good sense tells him "it is always as well to have a look at your captain before irrevocably committing yourself into his hands." But Captain Ahab, for some mysterious reason, refuses to be seen. This is clearly a warning, but Ishmael's failure to take it means that the ego's descent into the unconscious will be guided by an unknown attitude or motivation. Ishmael represses his sense of danger.

> When a man suspects any wrong, it sometimes happens that if he be already involved in the matter, he insensibly strives to cover up his suspicions even from himself. And much this way it was with me. I said nothing, and tried to think nothing. [Chapter 20]

The conscious sense of warning, having been repressed, is now relegated to the unconscious, but this is not the end of it. The warning returns personified in the ragged figure of Elijah, who accosts Ishmael and cautions him against Captain Ahab. The Biblical Elijah was the prophet of Yahweh who confronted the idolatrous Ahab and his wife, Jezebel [1 Kings: 17–19], but even this strange coincidence fails to provoke Ishmael's serious reflection. He dismisses Elijah as "cracked" and disregards the warning a second time.

The voyage begins on Christmas Day—the current form of the age-old festival of the winter solstice. Calendar symbolism is here combined with the symbolic meaning of the voyage. The winter solstice, long before Christ, was celebrated as the birthday of the sun. On this date, the darkest day of the year, the old sun reaches its nadir, and the new sun, a new light, is born out of the darkness and death of the old. This natural phenomenon reflects the death of an old psychological ruling principle and the birth of a new one. In Christian symbolism Christ is the new sun bringing salvation. The Pequod's Christmas sailing suggests that the center of dramatic action is shifting from one principle figure to another. Up to this point, Ishmael, identified with the ego, has been the central figure; from here to the end of the book the focus of attention will be Captain Ahab. Ishmael remains the narrator but assumes a subordinate position. Ahab is the newborn sun, the new dynamic principle emerging from the unconscious to direct the coming voyage.

In Chapters 26 and 27, the officers of the Pequod are introduced. There are four: Captain Ahab, First Mate Starbuck, Second Mate Stubb, and Third Mate Flask—a fourfold hierarchial structure suggesting Jung's four functions of the personality. The order of rank among the Pequod's officers establishes the relative development of the psychic function each represents. Ahab, as captain, stands for the superior function, which is thinking, as we shall see later after we have examined his three subordinate officers.

The first mate is Starbuck. He represents the auxiliary function. Starbuck is the name of an actual famous Nantucket family of wealthy whaling captains. Hence, the name carries associations of solid, responsible, successful functioning. This is also borne out by Melville's description: "This Starbuck seemed prepared to endure for long ages to come . . . his interior vitality was warranted to do well in all climates . . . a staid, steadfast man." [Chapter 26] The psychic function he represents is, in other words, well developed, well adapted, and differentiated. But which function is it? The following passage gives the answer:

> Yet, for all his hardy sobriety and fortitude, there were certain qualities in him which at times affected, and in some cases seemed well nigh to overbalance all the rest. Uncommonly conscientious for a seaman, and endued with a deep natural reverence, the wild watery loneliness of his life did therefore strongly incline him to superstitions; but to that sort of superstition, which in some organizations seems rather to spring, somehow, from intelligence than from ignorance. Outward portents and inward presentiments were his. [Chapter 26]

Outward portents and inward presentiments are the marks of the intuitive function.

Starbuck is a careful man. Both his father and his brother had been killed hunting whales (linking him with Ahab, who also has memories of a maiming encounter with a whale, and with Melville, who had lost his own father and brother). Starbuck's reaction to these tragedies is a realistic, adapted one: "I am here in this critical ocean to kill whales for my living, not to be killed by them for theirs," testifying to a high level of development for the function the first mate represents, intuition.

Stubb is third in command on the Pequod, a "good-humored, easy and careless" man. Thoughts of death, if he has any, are easily dispelled by a good dinner. He is an inveterate pipe-smoker "and as in time of cholera, some people go about with a camphorated handkerchief to their mouths; so, likewise, against all mortal tribulations, Stubb's tobacco smoke might have operated as a sort of disinfectant agent." [Chapter 27] This describes the sensation type—on a relatively undeveloped level, to be sure—a good dinner and a full pipe sufficing to keep him comfortably related to life. Later in the book, Ahab remarks of Starbuck and Stubb, "Ye two are the opposite poles of one thing. Starbuck is Stubb reversed, and Stubb is Starbuck." [Chapter 123] This observation corresponds to the psychological fact that sensation and intuition are opposite poles of the perceptive faculty.

Flask, the third mate, is the last of the four in order of rank, hence, according to our scheme, the representative of the inferior or least developed function. Accordingly, his personality description is brief. The inferior function, because of its being largely unconscious, is always the hardest for one to understand and describe; it remains rather vague and unformed. We are told only that Flask was "very pugnacious concerning whales . . . [he] somehow seemed to think that the great Leviathans had personally and hereditarily affronted him; and therefore it was a sort of point of honor with him to destroy them whenever encountered." [Chapter 27] An attitude of personal offense requiring satisfaction bespeaks a primitive, undeveloped feeling function. Flask seems to be emotionally challenging the whale to a duel in order to rectify an offense to his personal honor. Like Ahab, he has been offended and seeks a sort of vengeance, although Flask's vengeful attitude is no more than the palest shadow of his captain's.

We might outline Melville's personality through the officers he created for the Pequod: thinking, his superior function; intuition, its well-developed auxiliary; sensation, a rather poorly developed third; and feeling, his fourth function, undifferentiated and inferior. *Moby-Dick* shows a striking lack of differentiated feeling. It is notable that the novel contains no significant female (anima) figure! And Melville's personal relationships and feeling adaptation were correspondingly precarious. Likewise, his relatively inferior sensation function was evident in his life—in his shaky relation to reality, requiring support by relatives.

Melville intended the voyage of the Pequod to represent the isolated individual's journey into his own depths.

> They were nearly all Islanders in the Pequod, *Isolatoes* too, I call such, not acknowledging the common continent of men, but each *Isolato* living on a separate continent of his own. Yet now, federated along one keel, what a set these Isolatoes were! An Anacharsis Clootz deputation from all the isles of the sea, and all the ends of the earth, accompanying Old Ahab in the Pequod to lay the world's grievances before that bar from which not very many of them ever came back. [Chapter 27]

As soon as the Pequod sets out to sea, we are introduced to such an *Isolato*, that mysterious figure, Bulkington, who is never mentioned again for the rest of the book. Having just completed a four-year voyage, he has immediately committed himself to another "tempestuous term." Port and land seem intolerable to him. He gives us our first view of that inflated attitude which strives restlessly to transcend human limits.

> Glimpses do ye seem to see of that mortally intolerable truth; that all
> deep, earnest thinking is but the intrepid effort of the soul to keep the
> open independence of her sea; while the wildest winds of heaven and
> earth conspire to cast her on the treacherous slavish shore?
>
> But as in landlessness alone resides the highest truth, shoreless, in-
> definite as God—so, better, is it to perish in that howling, infinite, than
> be ingloriously dashed upon the lee, even if that were safety! For
> worm-like, then, oh! who would craven crawl to land! [Chapter 23]

His disdain of land signifies a renunciation of the structure and established categories of consciousness in favor of the infinite, boundless qualities of the collective unconscious. While this can be a noble
choice, it can also be rash and inflated if one neglects the realistic
limitations of human existence. Bulkington can be considered a variant of the attitude more fully developed in Ahab. They both manifest heroism in a desperate and one-sided form. Theirs is an extreme,
unbalanced courage, the reciprocal of Ishmael's initial depressive and
equally unbalanced escapism. Later, Starbuck, the Pequod's most
balanced personality, expresses the proper relation between courage
and caution:

> 'I will have no man in my boat,' said Starbuck, 'who is not afraid of a
> whale!' By this he seemed to mean, not only that the most reliable and
> useful courage was that which arises from the fair estimation of the
> encountered peril, but that an utterly fearless man is a far more dan-
> gerous comrade than a coward. [Chapter 26]

In the coming voyage, Ahab is to demonstrate the truth of this remark.

The regressive counterpart to Bulkington's doctrine that "in landlessness alone resides the highest truth" is the passive inflation of Ishmael's phantasy while standing watch at the masthead:

> Let me make a clean breast of it here, and frankly admit that I kept
> but sorry guard. With the problem of the universe revolving in me,
> how could I—being left completely to myself at such a thought-engen-
> dering altitude,—how could I but lightly hold my obligations to ob-
> serve all whaleships' standing orders, 'Keep your weather eye open,
> and sing out every time.' . . . lulled into such an opium-like listless-
> ness of vacant, unconscious reverie is this absent-minded youth by the
> blending cadence of waves with thoughts, that at last he loses his
> identity; takes the mystic ocean at his feet for the visible image of that
> deep, blue, bottomless soul, pervading mankind and nature; and every

strange, half-seen, gliding, beautiful thing that eludes him; every dimly-discovered, uprising fin of some undiscernable form, seems to him the embodiment of those elusive thoughts that only people the soul by continually flitting through it. In this enchanted mood, thy spirit ebbs away to whence it came; becomes diffused through time and space; like Cranmer's sprinkled Pantheistic ashes, forming at last a part of every shore the round globe over.

There is no life in thee, now, except that rocking life imparted by a gently rolling ship; by her, borrowed from the sea; by the sea, from the inscrutable tides of God. But while this sleep, this dream is on ye, move your foot or hand an inch; slip your hold at all; and your identity comes back in horror. Over Descartian vortices you hover. And perhaps, at mid-day, in the fairest weather, with one half-throttled shriek you drop through that transparent air into the summer sea, no more to rise for ever. Heed it well, ye Pantheists! [Chapter 35]

This is a beautiful description of the inflated state of passive identification with the unconscious. It occurs at a height, a "thought-engendering altitude," in other words, at a precarious remoteness from concrete reality. To be too high signifies an identification with airy spirit and a separation from material realities, where one is exposed to the danger of an abrupt destructive fall. There is a similar image in *White Jacket*, Chapter 92, when the hero falls from the topmost rigging into the sea and goes through a death and rebirth experience, freeing him from the accursed white jacket which symbolizes inflated purity and innocence. In *Redburn*, too, Melville describes an ascent of the mainmast at midnight and a fear of ". . . falling—falling—falling, as I have felt when the nightmare has been on me." [Chapter 16] These images suggest that Melville may have had nightmares of falling. Arvin states definitely that Melville suffered hysophobia (fear of heights).[2]

Fear of heights and dreams of falling, flying, or being at a frightening altitude carry a specific psychological meaning. They indicate that one has an inflated, unrealistic conscious attitude which is identified with spirit, that one is off the ground, and hence in a precarious relation to reality. The inflation is also an alienation insofar as being at a height separates one both from his fellows and from the earthy realities of one's own being. A fall is necessary, but if it is too abrupt, or if the dissociation is too great, the descent can be a disaster.

[2] Arvin, *op. cit.*, p. 115.

7 CAPTAIN AHAB

WHEN, after some days at sea, Captain Ahab finally appears on deck, we meet one of the most significant figures in American literature. He is a giant enigmatic figure who contains aspects of all the world's major myths and is himself a genuine and original myth.[1] Like Job, Oedipus, and Faust, Ahab speaks to all men. But he speaks best to those whose culture and idiom he shares; for Americans, the tragic figure of Ahab merits close scrutiny.

Being a product of Melville's imagination, Ahab has obvious connections with Melville's personal life and attitudes, some of which will be pointed out, but they are not the main matter. Ahab was born from the deep mythological layers of the collective psyche, a modern self-revelation of the collective psyche; he thus speaks to all contemporary men. Divine revelation did not terminate abruptly two thousand years ago. New mythological messages continue to emerge from the archetypal psyche and are transmitted through certain creative minds chosen as mouthpieces. Melville was such a mouthpiece, and the mythical figure of Ahab such a message.

The first aspect of Ahab to consider is his name. It means "the brother is father" or, alternatively, "the father's brother or uncle." Both meanings have significance in Melville's life, for his father died when he was twelve, his older brother Gansevoort taking over the role of father; and Melville's uncle, Peter Gansevoort, was to a large extent the real father of his family even before Allan Melville died. Not only did Uncle Peter frequently save Allan from financial difficulties with gifts and loans, but also Melville's mother as much as admits in her letters that she loved her brother Peter more than

---

[1] Walter Weber gives him this high praise: "Without further ceremony we may place Ahab among the greatest creations of all literature; he has a peculiar kinship with them all, but especially with the Greek Prometheus and the Miltonic Satan. One cannot on that account speak of borrowing, for this fruit of the deep art of symbolism is a supreme literary achievement, such as succeeds spontaneously and for only the greatest artists at the height of their powers." Weber, *Herman Melville, eine stilitische Untersuchung* (Basel: Philographischer Verlag, 1937). Cited in *Moby-Dick*, Mansfield and Vincent, eds., (New York: Hendricks House, 1962), p. 641.

her husband.[2] It is evident from the available material that Melville's father felt himself unmanned by his stronger brother-in-law, both in his inability to support his own family and in the affections of his wife and children. This state of affairs was bound to have its effects on the psychic atmosphere of Melville's childhood. It may have been as significant as his father's actual death.

In Judaic mythology, Ahab is an idolatrous backslider, a traitor to the covenant with Yahweh. A ninth-century B.C. king of Israel, the Biblical Ahab married Jezebel and, under her influence, permitted the idolatrous worship of Baal. The prophet Elijah denounced him, prophesying his downfall, for Baal and his mother consort, Astarte, were the major deities of the Phoenician matriarchal religion which the patriarchal religion of Yahweh opposed. Ahab is thus the prototype of the heretic. That Melville too was a heretic there can be no doubt. An entire book has been written to demonstrate his opposition to the orthodox religion of his day.[3]

What Melville thought of orthodoxies of all kinds is revealed in a passage from Chapter 69 commenting on the fact that the foam and white spray around the floating carcass of a dead whale is sometimes mistaken for breakers on rocks and recorded so in the ship's log:

> And for years afterwards, perhaps, ships shun the place; leaping over it as silly sheep leap over a vacuum, because their leader originally leaped there when a stick was held. There's your law of precedents; there's your utility of traditions; there's the story of your obstinate survival of old beliefs never bottomed on the earth, and now not even hovering in the air! There's orthodoxy!

The quest that leads one into the unconscious is heretical in its very nature. It cannot occur until one has lost his conscious allegiance to the collective religious symbols. The quest for individual religious experience invariably stems from Ishmael-like feelings of being an outsider, of being no longer comfortably contained by the collective, traditional, dogmatic symbolism. Ahab and Ishmael are the two sides of the heretical outsider. Ishmael the passive victim, Ahab the active rebel.

One of the important differences between the patriarchal religion

[2] Leyda, *op. cit.*, i, 54.
[3] Lawrance Thompson, *Melville's Quarrel with God* (Princeton, N.J.: Princeton University Press, 1952).

of Yahweh and the matriarchal nature religion of Baal is their contrasting attitudes toward images. Judaism, like Protestant Christianity, is opposed to the use of religious imagery. The commandment in Exodus 20:4, "You shall not make yourself a graven image, or any likeness of anything that is in heaven above, or that is in the earth beneath, or that is in the water under the earth," derives from the profound patriarchal antipathy toward the image-making powers of the psyche, the imagination, which has its roots in the maternal unconscious. We can say that one of the meanings idolatry carries in the Judeo-Christian context is the honoring of imagination, of spontaneous images from the unconscious. And this will be one of the meanings carried by the idolatrous Ahab. He will represent the artistic personality who sails the boundless sea of the imagination, creating graven images, against the injunction of the patriarchal god.

The taboo against images exists for good reasons. It is an aspect of the incest taboo. Imagination has its dangers; it draws libido away from the real world. For the immature ego, imagination easily can become wish-fulfilling phantasy and an escape from reality adaptation. Therefore, during a certain phase of ego development, it is absolutely necessary to depreciate the unconscious, the maternal womb of the ego, which is also the source of imagination. The conscious personality must separate itself from its origins if it is to achieve some measure of autonomy. This is the goal of all patriarchal initiation. The artist seems to have never completed this patriarchal initiation. In him, the door to the maternal unconscious with its rich store of images that feed the imagination remains open. He never gives complete allegiance to the masculine principle, but rather maintains an ambiguous relation to the feminine. In the Hebrew canon itself, in Numbers 21:5–9, there is a most interesting exception to the injunction against graven images:

> And the people spoke against God and against Moses, "Why have you brought us up out of Egypt to die in the wilderness? For there is no food and no water, and we loathe this worthless food!" Then the Lord sent fiery serpents among the people, and they bit the people, so that many people of Israel died. And the people came to Moses, and said, "We have sinned, for we have spoken against the Lord and against you; pray to the Lord, that he take away the serpents from us." So Moses prayed for the people. And the Lord said to Moses, "Make a

fiery serpent, and set it on a pole; and everyone who is bitten, when he sees it, shall live." So Moses made a bronze serpent, and set it on a pole; and if a serpent bit any man, he would look at the bronze serpent and live.

Yahweh is here contradicting his own commandment against making images. The bronze serpent, an image made by man, counteracts the destructive effects of the fiery serpents made and sent by God. The image-making power of man, his imagination, thus has a healing effect on damage inflicted by God—a most instructive lesson. In psychological terms, it is saying that the destructive effects of the unconscious can be healed by seeing the image of the agency of the hurt. The fiery serpents are the anger and resentment that bit the Israelites and poisoned them; to see an image of what has bitten one exteriorizes the unconscious affect and brings about a separation between it and the ego. This is equivalent to an increase of consciousness, which is the healing factor.[4]

The source of both the hurt and the healing is the same, the transpersonal psyche. Yahweh sent the serpents in the first place, and he also advised how their damaging effects could be cured. This corresponds to the paradoxical description of the alchemical Mercurius,[5]

[4] Another example of the healing power of images is found in I Samuel 6. The Philistines had captured the ark of the Covenant, and the appropriation of this sacred object had caused a plague of tumors (perhaps bubonic plague) among them. "And the Philistines called for the priests and the diviners and said, 'What shall we do with the ark of the Lord? Tell us with what we shall send it to its place.' They said, 'If you send away the ark of the God of Israel, do not send it empty, but by all means return him a guilt offering. Then you will be healed, and it will be known to you why his hand does not turn away from you.' And they said, 'What is the guilt offering that we shall return to him?' They answered, 'Five golden tumors and five golden mice, according to the number of the Philistines; for the same plague was upon all of you and upon your lords. *So you must make images of your tumors and images of your mice that ravage the land, and give glory to the God of Israel!*" [I Sam. 6:2–5] (Italics mine.)

[5] Mercurius says of himself, "I am the poison-dripping dragon. . . . My water and fire destroy and put together. . . . if you do not have exact knowledge of me, you will destroy your five senses with my fire. From my spout there comes a spreading poison that has brought death to many. . . . I contain the light of nature; I am dark and light; I come forth from heaven and earth; I am known and yet do not exist at all; by virtue of the sun's rays all colors shine in me, and all metals. I am the carbuncle of the sun, the most noble purified earth, through which you may change copper, iron, tin, and lead into gold." Quoted in C. G. Jung, *Alchemical Studies*, CW 13 (Princeton, N.J.: Princeton University Press, 1968), par. 267.

who is both poison and panacea. Yahweh and Mercurius both represent the objective psyche, whose energies are poisoning when they bite the ego, causing it to identify with them and act them out, but healing when the ego can experience them objectively, as images which promote consciousness. We are released from the poison of an affect if we can see the image that lies behind it.

Moses' brazen serpent symbolizes man's basic need for images. Man's life experience becomes bearable to the extent that he can view the image which lies behind it, because the image conveys consciousness and meaning. Hence we hunger for images; they are as vitally necessary for the psyche as food is for the body. For the individual, healing images come from dreams and imagination; collectively, they are supplied by fiction, drama, and art.

Yahweh's ambivalent attitude toward graven images is paralleled by his ambiguity in placing the tree of knowledge in the Garden of Eden and then forbidding Adam and Eve to eat of it. If they were to eat of it, they would "be like God," and so it is with the discovery of one's own image-creating powers. It is a Promethean act, an enhancement of the individual personality, but also an infringement on the prerogatives of the deity, a violation of a taboo.

There is obviously also a connection with Melville's own psychology. He was aware of the arrogance and audacity of his own creative powers, but permitted them, as Ishmael permitted Ahab, to take him on a reckless, heroic voyage into the unconscious. And it is not unlikely that Melville's creation of *Moby-Dick*, like Moses' brazen serpent, was the instrument of his own ultimate healing.

When Captain Ahab first appears on deck, we are told about a strange scar he bears:

> Threading its way out from among his grey hairs, and continuing right down one side of his tawny scorched face and neck, till it disappeared in his clothing, you saw a slender rod-like mark, lividly whitish. It resembled that perpendicular seam sometimes made in the straight, lofty trunk of a great tree when the upper lightning tearingly darts down it, and without wrenching a single twig, peels and grooves out the bark from top to bottom, ere running off into the soil, leaving the tree still greenly alive, but branded. [Chapter 28]

It is uncertain whether this scar is a birthmark, a hereditary predisposition, or the result of "an elemental strife at sea," that is, of an environmental trauma. This doubt may correspond to Melville's uncertainty as to whether his own destiny was predetermined prior to birth or caused by the trauma of his personal experience. Here is the heredity versus environment dispute in a nutshell. One can never be sure whether our psychological defects and peculiarities have been conditioned by our early experience or whether they are innate and predetermined, built into our destiny, as it were. At any rate, Captain Ahab is a marked man.

To be marked by God is to be set apart in some special way by the touch of the deity. Much later in the book, when Ahab is addressing the corpusants, he says, "Oh! thou clear spirit of clear fire, whom on these seas I as Persian once did worship, till in the sacramental act so burned by thee that to this hour I bear the scar." [Chapter 119] To have come too close to the numinous energies of the psyche means one will be permanently affected. It is an ambiguous matter to be marked by God. On the one hand, this image lies behind the notion of belonging to the elect or the chosen people; on the other, it reminds us of Cain.

In *Omoo*, Melville describes another marked man, a renegade white man who has gone native:

A renegado from Christendom and humanity—a white man in South Sea girdle, and tattooed in the face. A broad blue band stretched across his face from ear to ear, and on his forehead was the taper figure of a blue shark. . . . Some of us gazed upon this man with a feeling akin to horror, no ways abated when informed that he had voluntarily submitted to this embellishment of his countenance. What an impress! Far worse than Cain's. . . . He told me his history. Thrown upon the world a foundling, his paternal origin was as much a mystery to him as the genealogy of Odin; and, scorned by everybody, he fled the parish workhouse when a boy, and launched upon the sea. He had followed it for several years, a dog before the mast, and now he had thrown it up forever. [Chapter 7]

This association connects Ahab with the renegade tendency which is a traitor to the values of civilization and consciousness. If one's early experiences have been too harsh, one has had no basis laid for an allegiance to society and the collective human enterprise; no safeguards exist against the regressive nihilism of primitive affect.

In the Book of Revelation, to be marked has an ominous connotation.

> If anyone worships the beast and its image, and receives a mark on his forehead or on his hand, he also shall drink the wine of God's wrath, poured unmixed into the cup of his anger, and he shall be tormented with fire and brimstone. [Rev. 14:9–10]

According to one version, Ahab's mark is a great longitudinal scar extending the full length of his body from head to toe. Such a scar would in effect separate his right side from his left. Since right and left symbolize the conscious and unconscious aspects of the psyche respectively, the implication would be that Ahab has an innate personality defect which tends to dissociate consciousness from the unconscious—his madness, of course, also demonstrates it. To some extent the dissociation of consciousness from the unconscious is a necessary precondition for the growth of consciousness. Innumerable myths tell us this. The ego must experience a separation from the original state of unconscious wholeness if it is to achieve any freedom. But however necessary this process is, the dissociation carries serious dangers of inflation and alienation from the source of one's being. The psychology of schizophrenia reveals these universal psychic dangers in magnified form. In a description of Emerson, Melville reveals the nature of his own split, projected onto Emerson:

> I could readily see in Emerson, notwithstanding his merit, a gaping flaw. It was the insinuation that had he lived in those days when the world was made, he might have offered some valuable suggestions. These men are all *cracked right across the brow*. And never will the pullers-down be able to cope with the builders-up. (Italics mine.)[6]

No objective observer could possibly call Emerson a puller-down. All his writings attempt to justify the nature of things. It was Melville who had suggestions as to how the world ought to have been created; the resentment that pulls down was his own.

In addition to the birthmark scar, Ahab carries another wound. He had lost a leg in an encounter with Moby Dick and was left with a monomaniacal desire to revenge himself on the white whale.

> It is not probable that this monomania in him took its instant rise at the precise time of his bodily dismemberment. Then, in darting at the monster, knife in hand, he had but given loose to a sudden, passionate,

[6] Metcalf, *op. cit.,* p. 59.

corporal animosity; and when he received the stroke that tore him, he probably felt the agonizing bodily laceration, but nothing more. Yet, when by this collision forced to turn home, and for long months of days and weeks, Ahab and anguish lay stretched together in one hammock, round in mid winter that dreary, howling Patagonian Cape; then it was, that his torn body and gashed soul bled into one another; and so interfusing, made him mad. [Chapter 41]

Here is a most striking image, "his torn body and gashed soul bled into one another." It is an image of union, consciousness and the unconscious interpenetrate one another. But the result, instead of wholeness, is madness. This is the unhappy consequence of the dissociative tendency represented by the longitudinal scar. The body bleeds into the soul; that is, the collective unconscious with its archetypal images streams into consciousness. Instead of relating to these images meaningfully, however, Ahab becomes identified with them, succumbs to inflation, and thus to madness.

What is the meaning of Ahab's loss of a leg? First of all, the presence of such an image in Melville's imagination indicates that he had suffered a profoundly crippling psychic trauma. The historical cause of this damage probably lies in Melville's relation to his parents. Relatively rejected by his mother, who favored his older brother, in his phantasy he imagined he had a stepmother. He was thus deprived of an adequate personal experience of the positive mother archetype.

His father experience was even more traumatic. Allan Melville was a weak man. While attempting to fulfill the social ambitions of his wife, he mismanaged his business affairs and became more and more dependent on the charity of his relatives. At the same time that he was moving to more sumptuous rented quarters, he was asking for loans from his father and his brother-in-law. He complained to his wife that she loved her brother more than him, as in fact she did. This same brother-in-law lectured him on how to bring up his children and, in the same letter, informed him that his (Allan's) son had told his uncle that he loved him more than he did his father. The personality of the father is a major factor in the psychological development of a boy; he is the first and most important figure to embody for his son the nature of masculinity. Through his relationship with an adequate father, a son first learns what it is to be a man and, through this experience, is able to incorporate a masculine attitude into his own personality. One of Melville's major traumata was his father's masculine inadequacy, mental breakdown, and subsequent death, followed by all its harsh consequences of poverty, appeals for charity, and disruption of education.

For a child to experience a parent's psychosis probably has a more disastrous effect than the parent's actual death. The child relies heavily on the parent's psychic integrity for his own sense of security. To witness the complete disintegration of the parent's personality is an appalling disaster which tears a hole out of the child's tender, undeveloped psyche. Melville describes poignantly how this experience effected him in his novel *Redburn:*

> Talk not of the bitterness of middle-age and after life; a boy can feel all that, and much more, when upon his young soul the mildew has fallen; and the fruit, which with others is only blasted after ripeness, with him is nipped in the first blossom and bud. And never again can such blights be made good; they strike in too deep, and leave such a scar that the air of Paradise might not erase it. And it is a hard and cruel thing thus in early youth to taste beforehand the pangs which should be reserved for the stout time of manhood, when the gristle has become bone, and we stand up and fight out our lives, as a thing tried before and foreseen; for then we are veterans used to sieges and battles, and not green recruits, recoiling at the first shock of the encounter. [Chapter 2]

One can reconstruct Melville's experience of his father from scattered passages in his writings. In *Redburn*, the hero says, "I had never dreamed of such a thing as doubting him [father]; for I always thought him a marvellous being, infinitely purer and greater than I was, who could not by any possibility do wrong, or say an untruth." [Chapter 7] Pierre feels similarly toward his dead father, until he discovers his father conceived an illegitimate child. Shattering disillusionment follows:

> Ay, Pierre, now indeed art thou hurt with a wound, never to be completely healed but in heaven; for thee, the before undistrusted moral beauty of the world is forever fled; for thee, thy sacred father is no more a saint; all brightness hath gone from thy hills, and all peace from thy plains; and now, now, for the first time, Pierre, Truth rolls a black billow through thy soul! Ah, miserable thou, to whom Truth, in her first tides, bears nothing but wrecks! [*Pierre*, Book III, Chapter 6]

It may be that Melville discovered some sexual indiscretion of his father; the latter did make many business trips to Paris. More likely, however, the disillusionment came from the realization of his father's general weakness.

When the parents are adequate to their task of incarnating and mediating the archetypal images of mother and father, the psyche's deeper numinous energies are buffered by being personalized in human forms. When there is a grave defect in the parents' psychology which prevents them from fulfilling this mediating function, a kind of hole is left in the child's psyche. This hole will expose the child, later in life, to violent eruptions of primitive, unmediated archetypal images, "a bleeding of the body into the soul." This is what happened to Melville. It accounts for his difficult, conflict-laden personal life—and also for the brilliant creative energies that made him a genius. Melville sensed this and thus could say, "All mental greatness is but disease." [Chapter 16] Again, at the end of the book, Ahab exclaims, "Oh, now I feel my topmost greatness lies in my topmost grief." [Chapter 135]

The life of the historical Jesus, so far as we can reconstruct it, probably involved some similar deprivation. He was undoubtedly an illegitimate child, without an experience of the personal father; this gap in his psyche would have opened him to a sense of direct, unmediated relationship to the archetypal father (God), with the natural consequence of experiencing himself as the son of God. Lesser degrees of this phenomenon are common. Behind the personal mother and father lie a priori, archetypal images of the suprapersonal parents, and whenever a child's parental relation is inadequate, phantasies of the "original" or "royal" parents are apt to emerge. Examples of this theme abound in fairy tales.

Psychic trauma and deprivation are not necessarily unmitigated evils. The connection between greatness and depth of vision on the one hand, and grief, morbidity, and suffering on the other, is a psychological fact. The development of individual consciousness—separation of the ego from the original state of *participation mystique*—unavoidably requires the enduring of a wound. The mythical images of a chained Prometheus gnawed by the vulture and of Christ crucified demonstrate this fact. The psychic wound can be not only a painful defect, but also a gateway to the transpersonal psyche. Frustration and suffering, up to the limits of the ego's capacity to assimilate them, can promote psychological growth. Beyond those limits it only destroys.

Ahab as the representative of Melville's superior function, thinking, needs further scrutiny. Melville's descriptions of the other three officers, Starbuck, Stubb, and Flask, make it quite definite that they refer to the functions of intuition, sensation, and feeling, respectively. Thus, by a process of elimination, if Ahab is to be the superior function, this must be thinking. But the picture given of Ahab does not completely support this conclusion. He is not a clear thinker. He seems rather to be a magnified, enraged version of Flask, the feeling function, whose chief characteristic is his feeling of vengeance against whales. Late in the book, Ahab says,

> "Ahab never thinks; he only feels, feels, feels; *that's* tingling enough for mortal man! to think's audacity. God only has that right and privilege. Thinking is, or ought to be, a coolness and a calmness; and our poor heart's throb, and our poor brains beat too much for that." [Chapter 135]

How ironic! Ahab speaks of audacity! This is reminiscent of the passage previously quoted from one of Melville's letters to Hawthorne,

> I stand for the heart. To the dogs with the head! I had rather be a fool with a heart, than Jupiter Olympus with his head. The reason the mass of men fear God, and at bottom dislike Him, is because they rather distrust His heart and fancy Him all brain like a watch.[7]

On the face of it, "I stand for the heart. To the dogs with the head!" suggests that Melville is a feeling type. In both these passages, however, thinking is associated with God, i.e., the highest value, which indicates that the thinking function is the most honored one and hence is inherently the superior function. Also, there is an intensity in the expression "To the dogs with the head" which makes one suspicious. As Ahab said to Starbuck, discrediting himself at the same time, "what is said in heat, that thing unsays itself." So Melville's heated exclamation unsays itself to the careful observer. He protests too much. Furthermore, this remark is similar to a passage in Shakespeare's *King Lear*, which Melville had marked at the time:[8] "Truth's

[7] Ibid., p. 109.
[8] Charles Olson, *Call Me Ishmael* (New York: Grove Press, 1947), p. 42.

a dog must to kennel." The similarity between Shakespeare's remark and Melville's suggests that the latter is cutting himself off from his own highest value, truth, when he says, "To the dogs with the head."

These considerations suggest Melville had an ambivalent relation to the thinking function. The figure of Ahab does not correspond clearly with the thinking function because of his wound and his contamination with the vengeance of the inferior feeling function, Flask. His predilection for thought, however, shows in his mock request to the carpenter: "I'll order a complete man after a desirable pattern . . . no heart at all, brass forehead, and about a quarter of an acre of fine brains." [Chapter 108] I conclude that Ahab represents Melville's *potentially* superior thinking function, which had suffered a developmental damage and had been maddeningly wounded. So, in *Moby-Dick* we have a picture of a particular psychological state, the dictatorship of a crippled superior function which continues to dominate the personality even after it has demonstrated its inadequacy to lead.

The tyranny of the superior function is a common problem in psychotherapy. For the sake of efficiency in adapting to life, a kind of psychological specialization which develops one function at the expense of others is unavoidable. At one phase of development, there is an inner tendency for psychic differentiation to proceed in this one-sided fashion. But modern society tremendously augments this inner tendency by giving all its rewards to specialization. The demands of psychological growth eventually require that the superior function's sovereignty be overthrown. Its particular viewpoint, or life orientation, is finally exhausted and must make way for other modes of experience still fresh and young and containing potential. When this point is reached, the inner situation is analogous to a country that needs to overthrow an old, outmoded regime. But power long held becomes entrenched and seldom abdicates voluntarily, and so it is with the superior function. The more it has lost its creative potential, the more tyrannical it is apt to become. Like an egocentric dictator, it functions as an autonomous partial-system that puts its own well-being ahead of the psychic organism as a whole. Primitive peoples, as described by Fraser, periodically killed their king ritually and replaced him with a young ruler; something similar must happen in the individual psyche if one is not to fall victim to the sterile inner tyranny of one's superior function. Ahab represents such a tyrannical superior function refusing to relinquish its power. When the time comes, and the laws of life demand the old ruler be sacrificed, the question arises, as with Ahab and his crew, whether or not the superior function will succeed in carrying the rest of the personality with it down to destruction.

8 AHAB AND MYTHOLOGY

MELVILLE CLEARLY means for Ahab to have universal relevance. Around his tragic hero, he weaves a rich network of symbolical and mythological allusions. In fact, the figure of Ahab assimilates to itself most of the major myths of the world. We have already noted Ahab's identification with the newborn sun in the facts that the Pequod sails on Christmas Day, the winter solstice, and, as the ship sails south, Ahab's increasing appearances on deck parallel the sun's increasing emergence. Ahab considers himself the sun's equal when he says, "Talk not to me of blasphemy, man; I'd strike the sun if it insulted me." [Chapter 36] In one of his aspects, Ahab belongs to that group of sun-heroes who, like the sun, are dismembered or swallowed by a monster in the west only to rise again newborn in the east. Like Ahab, "sun-heroes often have a limb missing";[1] or, alternatively, they may have a weak or wounded foot. Oedipus, for instance, who has certain connections with the sun-hero, has a name meaning "swollen foot."[2]

The Egyptian Osiris was a sun-hero with parallels in Ahab. The myth of Osiris has numerous, conflicting variations, but its basic outline is as follows: Osiris was a culture hero of the Egyptians.

[1] Frobenius. Quoted by Jung in *Symbols of Transformation*, par. 356, note 50.

[2] The image of the damaged or amputated extremity comes up elsewhere in Melville's writings. In *Mardi*, the savage Samoa lost an arm in a fight to save his ship from pirates. He is compared with other amputated warrior-heroes, such as Nelson, Anglesea, Arnold, etc. (*Mardi*, Chapter 24). In *Typee*, Tommo has a swollen leg which cripples him throughout his stay on the primitive island of Nukuheva. The leg begins to heal only after his rescue by a whaling ship. Tommo's crippled leg can be seen as the psychological effect of a regression to the primitive, infantile state represented by the savage island. It is a condition of symbolic incest which makes Tommo an Oedipus (swollen foot).

Through treachery, his wicked brother Set (or Typhon) enclosed him in a chest and threw him into the sea. The chest washed up on the Syrian coast at Byblos, where a huge tree grew around and enclosed it. Osiris' sister and wife, Isis, found the tree and brought the trunk of it back to Egypt. Again Set captured Osiris from the tree and this time dismembered him, spreading his fragments far and wide. The faithful Isis searched the earth for his scattered pieces and put Osiris together again. One piece, his phallus, could not be found because it had been swallowed by a fish. To take its place, Isis fashioned a wooden phallus. Although Osiris could not be restored fully to life, Isis conceived by him a son, Horus, who when he reached manhood avenged his father's murder by defeating Set.

The myth represents the transformation of libido. Osiris is the old sun fated to be dismembered, and Horus is the new sun, the rebirth and rejuvenation of psychic energy on a new level. Much in this myth is helpful in understanding Ahab's symbolic meaning. It is prophesied in Chapter 37 that Ahab will be dismembered—the fate of Osiris—and a partial dismemberment has already occurred. One commentator on Melville,[3] seeing the connection between Ahab and Osiris, believes that Melville purposely chose the Egyptian myth as the prototype for Ahab. This seems doubtful. It is evident that Melville was aware of parallels between his story and Egyptian mythology, but he also makes explicit comparisons with many other mythologies—Hebrew, Indian, Greek, and Christian. Rather than having consciously chosen any particular model to imitate, it is more likely that the archetypal images which emerged spontaneously from Melville's unconscious derive from the universal, collective psyche common to all men. Hence, the myth of Ahab would have discernible analogies to the myths of all ages and all places. The myth of Osiris, too, is a particular variation on a universal theme, which also gave rise to such figures as Dionysus, Attis, Adonis, Christ, and the innumerable myths of the hero's fight with the dragon.

In all its ramifications, the myth of Osiris carries a profound and complex symbolism.[4] A myth of rebirth and transformation, it symbolizes the development of the individual personality. Osiris has

[3] H. Bruce Franklin, *The Wake of the Gods* (Stanford, Cal.: Stanford University Press, 1963), pp. 53–98.

[4] See Erich Neumann's discussion of Osiris in *The Origins and History of Consciousness*. Bollingen Series XLII. (New York: Pantheon, 1954), pp. 220–56.

been variously identified with the spirit of vegetation, the fructify-ing flood of the Nile, the course of the sun, Apollo, and the Lord of the Underworld; he is thus a symbol of libido, the natural generative energy of the psyche, undergoing a process of transformation or development through dissolution and reconstitution. Ahab, like Osi-ris, is fated to be dismembered, and his whole compulsive search for the white whale is an unconscious drive toward that fate.

Osiris represents a phase of personality development which must undergo dismemberment in order to be reborn on another level. This phase is that of the ego still largely identified with the original state of wholeness, the primordial Self, an inflated, unrealistic state in which the individual unconsciously assumes that he is the center of the universe and is identified with God. In the myth, it is the god Osiris who is dismembered, but in the individual experiencing this process, it is that part of his own personality identified with God, the objective psyche, that is being dismembered.

Although consciously Ahab seeks to destroy Moby-Dick, the un-conscious effect of his compulsion is to drive him to his destiny of dismemberment. In his arrogant hybris, Ahab personifies that part of the ego identified with the Self; and if progressive differentiation between the ego and the Self is to develop, the ego-Self identity (Ahab) must undergo dissolution. This fate is motivated by power-ful energies of psychic growth, which accounts for the strong sense of predetermined destiny Ahab feels.

As defier of the gods, Ahab has associations with Prometheus. Melville says of Ahab,

> God help thee, old man, thy thoughts have created a creature in thee; and he whose intense thinking thus makes him a Prometheus; a vulture feeds upon that breast for ever; that vulture the very creature he creates. [Chapter 44]

The Prometheus myth symbolizes the necessary act of inflation or hybris which must be risked in each new step in the growth of con-sciousness. To steal the fire of the gods is a crime which must be paid for by the torment of the vulture. The solar fire symbolizes a new acquisition of consciousness; it is also the creative capacity it-self—the primal energy of the objective psyche. If that energy is to be made available for conscious use, a price must be paid. For Mel-ville, as for all creative geniuses, the myth of Prometheus is especially applicable. Before the writing of *Moby-Dick*, Sophia Hawthorne said of him, "The freshness of primeval nature is in that man and the true Promethean fire. . . ."[5] The tragic figure of suffering Ahab "with crucifixion in his face" is the symbolic representation of the price Melville had to pay for his gift of genius. At the same time, the figure of Ahab takes its place with Prometheus as an original mythical expression of the price we all pay in striving for greater consciousness.

Another important mythological connection associates Ahab with Christ. Several references make this clear. The Pequod sets sail on Christmas Day. At his first appearance on deck, "Ahab stood before them with a crucifixion in his face; in all the nameless regal overbearing dignity of some mighty woe." [Chapter 28] In Chapter 37, Ahab speaks of wearing the "Iron Crown of Lombardy." This crown was used traditionally at the coronation of the Holy Roman Emperor, and according to legend was forged from the nails of Christ's cross.

Further proof of the association between Ahab and Christ is found by comparing Ahab with Pierre. A careful reading of *Pierre* can leave no doubt that its central figure represents the same one-sided, heaven-storming attitude as does Ahab, and Pierre is clearly equated with Christ in many passages. To give just two examples, speaking of Pierre's determination the author says, "Thus in the enthusiast to Duty, the heaven-begotten Christ is born." [Book 5, Chapter 5] And again, shortly later, Pierre exclaims, "May heaven new-string my soul, and confirm me in the Christ-like feeling I first felt." [Book 5, Chapter 6]

At first sight it may seem incredible that mad, vengeful Ahab could be related to Christ, the apotheosis of love, purity, and innocence. But this is just one more example of the paradoxical play of opposites that runs throughout *Moby-Dick*. If the white whale is equated with evil, Ahab, its antagonist, must be equated with good, even with Christ Himself. At least this will be the way Ahab sees his own efforts. He is identified with Christ, the bright son of God, and in that inflated identification, he succumbs to an identification with its opposite, Satan, the dark son of God. Thus, it always is with

5 Metcalf, *op. cit.*, p. 90.

moral onesidedness. The greatest atrocities are performed by those most consciously self-righteous.

Ahab is an amputated man. His original wholeness has been violated and dismembered. In alchemical symbolism, one phase of the transformation process is represented by a lion with his paws cut off.[6] Osiris and Dionysus were dismembered; Attis and Adonis were castrated; Adam was cut off from the complete life in the garden of Eden; Oedipus was blinded; Christ was crucified—all these myths have a thread of common meaning. Man is born in a state of original wholeness; like the animals he is at one with the source of his being. The ego, in the course of its development, must separate itself from the archetypal psyche. This process in its very nature is a tearing, wounding dismemberment, for the original state of unconscious wholeness must be torn apart if a higher level of conscious development is to be achieved. The agony of Prometheus chained to the Caucacus, of Adam's sweat and toil, and of Christ's crucifixion all portray the consequences of the tearing apart of the conscious and unconscious portions of the personality. Ishmael and Ahab are representations of the same process. Both have been alienated from their original wholeness and their original source of satisfaction. Ishmael's reaction is passive escape and thoughts of suicide. Ahab's reaction is resentful defiance. He vows that he will "dismember his dismemberer." [Chapter 37] He cannot grant the existence of a higher psychic authority than the ego.

Ahab is a study in the psychology of resentment. His image serves as a mirror, showing the true nature of our own resentments. Everyone has this problem, his inner Ahab, his monomania, whose means are sane but whose motive and object are mad. Resentment that strives to get even, that inflicts one hurt for another, that asserts one's personal power over anything that challenges it, or that withdraws in sullen, wounded majesty, disdaining to communicate with a world that doesn't recognize its sovereignty, these are expressions of the Ahab in every soul.

Resentment—in its various manifestations—is perhaps the central problem of psychological development and psychotherapy. Jung writes,

A deep resentment seems to dwell in man's breast against the brutal

[6] Jung, *Psychology and Alchemy*, Fig. 4.

law that once separated him from instinctive surrender to his desires and from the beautiful harmony of animal nature.[7]

This is the resentment at our loss of original unconscious wholeness; it is resentment against the specifically human task of developing consciousness, a sacrificial task requiring the acceptance of dismemberment as part of the process.

Ahab demonstrates the fact that resentment is an inflation, an identification of the ego with the Self. Its eventual consequence is a fall, a catastrophe, but prior to that there may be evidence of an extraordinary energy, a demonic drive that taps nonpersonal psychic energy for a narrow, personal end. This was the case with Ahab.

> Far from having lost his strength, Ahab to that one end, did now possess a thousand fold more potency than ever he had sanely brought to bear upon any one reasonable object. [Chapter 41]

James Kirsch sees Ahab as a prefiguration of the twentieth-century dictatorships. He also speaks of an identification between ego and Self which

> produces a remarkable increase of the intellect and of power over other human beings but which is dehumanizing. Thus demonized, the ego subjects individuals and groups to its own wishes and goals, assimilates them into its own system and estranges them from themselves morally and in every other way. Such a *Gott-ahnlichkeit* ultimately leads to the destruction of the ego and of all who willingly accept this power. Individually this means psychosis, collectively a violent breakdown of the social order.[8]

One night while Ahab is moodily pacing the deck, Stubb comes up apologetically to remind him that the pounding of his ivory leg on the deck keeps the sailors below awake. Ahab replies in angry irritation, "down dog and kennel!" Stubb retires, feeling kicked, and having a strong urge to kick back. Then he has a dream which he later recounts to Flask:

> Such a queer dream, King-Post, I never had. You know the old man's ivory leg, well, I dreamed he kicked me with it; and when I tried to

---

[7] *Symbols of Transformation,* par. 351.
[8] James Kirsch, "The Problem of Dictatorship as Represented in Moby Dick," in *Current Trends in Analytical Psychology,* (London: Tavistock, 1961), p. 273.

kick back, upon my soul, my little man, I kicked my leg right off!
And then, presto! Ahab seemed a pyramid, and I, like a blazing fool,
kept kicking at it. [Chapter 31]

There is more to the dream, but that is the gist of it. With a few
changes it could have been Ahab's dream. As Ahab kicks at a stony
fact of nature, the white whale, Stubb kicks at the reality of Ahab
and, like Ahab, loses a leg (in the dream). Melville might actually
have dreamed this; it is consistent with other imagery in *Moby-Dick*
and elsewhere in his work.

What does a pyramid mean to Melville? There is a hint in the
notebooks he kept during his trip through Egypt and the Near East
in 1856–57. After seeing the pyramids, he wrote, "A feeling of awe
and terror came over me . . . I shudder at the idea of the ancient
Egyptians. It was in these pyramids that the idea of Jehovah was
born. A terrible mixture of the cunning and the awful. Moses was
learned in all the lore of the Egyptians."[9] Evidently, Melville sub-
scribed to the notion that Mosaic monotheism was of Egyptian
origin. At any rate, in this passage Melville associates pyramids with
the birthplace of Yahweh, making it the stony, immutable deity itself that Stubb is kicking against—the same object against which
Ahab is venting his fury. In Melville's poem, "The Great Pyramid,"[10] we find further associations:

> Your masonry—and is it man's?
> More like some Cosmic artisan's.
> Your courses as in strata rise,
> > Like Grampians.
>
> Far slanting up your sweeping flank
> Arabs with Alpine goats may rank,
> And there they find a choice of passes
> Even like to dwarfs that climb the masses
> > Of glaciers blank.
>
> Shall lichen in your crevice fit?
> Nay, sterile all and granite-knit:
> Weather nor weather-strain ye rue,
> But aridly you cleave the blue
> > As lording it.

[9] Leyda, *op. cit.*, p. 542.
[10] Melville, *Collected Poems*, p. 254f.

Morn's vapor floats beneath your peak,
Kites skim your side with pinion weak;
To sand-storms battering, blow on blow,
Raging to work your overthrow,
    You—turn the cheek.

All elements unmoved you stem,
Foursquare you stand and suffer them:
Time's future infinite you dare,
While, for the past, 'tis you that wear
    Eld's diadem.

Slant from your inmost lead the caves
And labyrinths rumored. These who braves
And penetrates (old palmers said)
Comes out afar on deserts dead
    And, dying, raves.

Craftsmen, in dateless quarries dim,
Stones formless into form did trim,
Usurped on Nature's self with Art,
And bade this dumb I AM to start,
    Imposing him.

In the first stanza the pyramid is likened to whales (Grampus is a species of whale), in the second to the blank icy walls of glaciers (discussed below), and in the sixth stanza the pyramid is purported to have deeply hidden caves and labyrinths which bring insanity to those who penetrate them, a clear image of the unconscious and the dangers it can hold.[11] Walter Bezanson has already noted[12] that the sixth stanza's reference to a raving death probably alludes to Melville's experience of his father's insanity and death. The final stanza clearly suggests that Melville's titanism, his heaven-storming tendency, refers to his effort as a creative artist to give form to the inner chaos, to give expression to the "dumb I AM."

[11] A passage in *Pierre* also links the pyramid with the unconscious (soul). "By vast pains we mine into the pyramid; by horrible gropings we come to the central room; with joy we espy the sarcophagus; but we lift the lid—and nobody is there! appallingly vacant as vast is the soul of a man!" (Book XXI, Chapter 1).

[12] In his introduction to Melville's *Clarel* (Chicago: Hendricks House, 1959), p. xvii.

As we have seen, the hero of *Pierre* reveals many similarities to Ahab. At one point, Pierre falls asleep and sees in his dream a precipitous mountain. (This dream too may well have been the author's.) At the base of the mountain is a group of heaven-assaulting Titans.

> The herded Titans now sprang to their feet; flung themselves up the slope; and anew battered at the precipice's unresounding wall. Foremost among them all, he saw a moss-turbaned, armless giant, who despairing of any other mode of wreaking his immitigable hate, turned his vast trunk into a battering ram, and hurled his own arched-out ribs again and yet again against the invulnerable steep. "Enceladus! it is Enceladus!"–Pierre cried out in his sleep. That moment the phantom faced him; and Pierre saw Enceladus no more; but on that Titan's armless trunk, his own duplicate face and features magnifiedly gleamed upon him with prophetic discomfiture and woe. [Book XXV, Chapter 5]

Enceladus, one of the Titans defeated by Zeus, in this dream is trying to regain his lost position in heaven. But the mountain is impregnable, and he can do no more than destroy himself in a suicidal attack against it. Like Ahab, Enceladus is mutilated, having lost his arms.

Another example of the theme occurs in a later poem entitled "The Berg (A Dream)."[13] Its first paragraph gives the basic content:

> I saw a ship of martial build
> (Her standards set, her brave apparel on)
> Directed as by madness mere
> Against a stolid iceberg steer,
> Nor budge it, though the infatuate ship went down.
> The impact made huge ice-cakes fall
> Sullen, in tons that crashed the deck;
> But that one avalanche was all—
> No other movement save the foundering wreck.

This is surely an actual dream of Melville's. Using different images, it presents the same basic content as Ahab's assault on the white whale, Stubb's dream of kicking the pyramid, and Enceladus' attack on the mountain of Zeus. Such dreams carry a warning. The ship, representing the dreamer's conscious life-orientation, is willfully

[13] Melville, *Collected Poems,* p. 203.

pursuing a suicidal course, deliberately ramming a solid iceberg.[14] According to all the usual criteria, this image indicates a grave maladaptation to reality. Such a dream brought to an analyst would cause him concern for the patient's sanity. We know Melville's sanity was in grave danger for several years after *Moby-Dick*. Melville, however, evidently did reflect on his dreams. In this case, he wrote a poem about one. Apparently, the message of this and other dreams did get through to him, since he did not suffer a total shipwreck, as did Nietzsche, although he came perilously close to it. These examples give us a fearful glimpse into the dream life of a major creative artist. The psychological risk which accompanied Melville's creative efforts is appalling.

The pyramid of Stubb's dream, the mountain of Pierre's dream, and the iceberg of Melville's dream are analogous images referring to the same symbolic fact. The pyramid associates to Yahweh, the mountain to Zeus, and, in the context of Melville's psychology, I understand the iceberg to represent the mystery of ultimate reality which with his creative imagination he attacked so valiantly. The dream makes clear how futile, indeed disastrous, that effort was for him personally. There is another way of looking at it, however. The ship's impact did break up a portion of the iceberg, causing an avalanche of ice-cakes. This image suggests that the purposeful collision of ship and iceberg, while fatal to the ship, may have had a long-range collective value.

Melville pitted the powers of his own creative imagination against the ultimate mystery of human existence. Although the effort was inevitably a failure and a personal catastrophe, some pieces of that icy mystery were broken off. The great bulk of the iceberg was diminished to some extent by the creative capacity to dismember a portion of it into meaningful symbolic images. Perhaps all original myth-making is of this nature. A collision against the impenetrable mystery of being may bring personal trauma or tragedy, but collec-

[14] Another image of willful shipwreck is found in *Pierre*. "Now he began to feel that in him, the thews of a Titan were forestallingly cut by the scissors of Fate. He felt as a moose hamstrung. . . . He seemed gifted with loftiness, merely that it must be dragged down to the mud. Still, the profound willfulness in him would not give up. Against the breaking heart, and the bursting head; against all the dismal lassitude, and deathful faintness and sleeplessness, and whirlingness, and craziness, still he like a demi-god bore up. His soul's ship foresaw the inevitable rocks, but resolved to sail on, and make a courageous wreck." (Book XXV, Chapter 3).

tively, given the image-making genius, it produces a new symbolic image to be added to the collective cultural consciousness.

Stubb takes his dream of kicking the pyramid seriously and learns from it. Open and flexible enough to hear its message, he remarks that the dream has "made a wise man of me." Stubb's wisdom ultimately became Melville's own.

In the next sequence, Ahab gathers all hands on deck to inform them of his vengeful plans to seek out Moby-Dick and destroy him. The power of his conviction is contagious. With true rabble-rousing technique—evoking hatred, then providing an enemy on which to vent the hatred—Ahab infects the whole crew with his madness. Only Starbuck raises an objection. When Ahab asks, "Wilt thou not chase the white whale? Art not game for Moby-Dick?" Starbuck replies,

> "I am game for his crooked jaw, and for the jaws of Death too, Captain Ahab, if it fairly comes in the way of the business we follow; but I came here to hunt whales, not my commander's vengeance. How many barrels will thy vengeance yield thee even if thou gettest it, Captain Ahab? It will not fetch thee much in our Nantucket market."
> [Chapter 36]

This is eminently reasonable, the typical reply of common sense and expediency. But precisely in its expedient reasonableness lies its weakness. The urgencies that fire men's souls are rarely matters of material expediency. The most ruthless dictators gain their power by making what can only be called, no matter how perverse, a spiritual appeal. They awaken in their followers the dynamism of an archetypal image, an ideal. Once awakened, such an image has tremendous power. It generates the capacity to sacrifice personal and material well-being to a sometimes astonishing degree, for it conveys a sense of nobility, a way of life that transcends the ego and its personal desires and creates a devotion to a suprapersonal purpose. Such a process is always operating in mass movements. Although, because they function through unconscious dynamisms, such movements are almost always disastrous, nevertheless the source of their energy is spiritual. Because they appeal to a psychic value, not a material one, they can be opposed only by spiritual means. The appeal to market value is never enough to deal with an activated archetype.

Ahab is able to sway his hearers so easily because he activates a latent archetypal pattern, the conflict of human consciousness against evil and the powers of darkness. When activated, such an image can release tremendous energies. Whether these energies work for good or ill depends upon the quality and extent of the human consciousness which mediates them. History's greatest atrocities have been perpetrated by men in the unconscious grip of this archetype. Ahab, possessed by this mythological motivation and its unconscious power, magically infects the less-developed personalities of his crew:

> My one cogged circle fits into all their various wheels, and they revolve. Or, if you will, like so many ant-hills of powder, they all stand before me; and I am their match. Oh, hard! that to fire others, the match itself must needs be wasting! [Chapter 37]

We can see why Starbuck's appeal to reasonable expediency is inadequate. Faced with a spiritual challenge, he has no adequate spiritual response. After his appeal to the values of the market place fails, he tries again. "To be enraged with a dumb thing, Captain Ahab, seems blasphemous." Now he is meeting Ahab on his own ground, the spirit. The reply, though, is still insufficient. Ahab carries more power because, however wrong he is, his conviction rests on greater life experience. He sees deeper than Starbuck. He has experienced the psychic meaning hidden in the outer world.

> "All visible objects, man, are but as pasteboard masks. But in each event—in the living act, the undoubted deed—there, some unknown but still reasoning thing puts forth the mouldings of its features from behind the unreasoning mask." [Chapter 36]

Ahab has gone too deep for Starbuck. The latter cannot equal his psychological experience and hence is mastered:

> My soul is more than matched; she's overmanned; and by a madman! Insufferable sting, that sanity should ground arms on such a field! I think I see his impious end; but feel that I must help him to it. Will I, nill I, the ineffable thing has tied me to him; tows me with a cable I have no knife to cut. [Chapter 38]

Thus rational consciousness acknowledges its impotence, and the autonomous complex personified by Ahab rushes toward its resolution.

9 THE MEANING OF THE WHALE

WITH THE CREW all committed to the destruction of Moby-Dick, we must now turn to the question: What is the meaning of this mighty whale, the central character of the book? The problem is that the whale has too many meanings. Melville has gone to great trouble to provide an almost boundless network of associations to amplify the image of the whale. The whale and its multitude of meanings becomes a Cretan labyrinth wherein one is almost sure to lose himself. The amplification process begins before the narrative itself in the extracts concerning whales that Melville has collected from the literature and mythologies of the world. This collection of general and mythological associations to the whale, together with much other evidence in the book proper, indicates that Melville had discovered on his own the amplification method and used it to gain entrance to the collective unconscious.

Amplification as developed by Jung is a fundamental procedure in the process of uncovering and analyzing the unconscious. According to this procedure, dreams and other psychic images are used to initiate a series of associations which enlarge the meaning of the initial image and provide it with a context. The method of amplification has two aspects, personal amplification and general amplification. The first step, personal amplification, is done by asking the patient to express his spontaneous feelings, thoughts, and memories pertaining to his personal life that come to mind concerning the given image. The totality of these personal associations to all the elements in a dream provide the personal context of the dream and often lead to a significant meaning. The second step is general amplification. This is done by the psychotherapist on the basis of his own knowledge. General amplification provides the collective, archetypal associations to the dream elements. It is here that the therapist's knowledge of the collective or objective psyche is put to use. When a dream contains an archetypal image or theme, the therapist demonstrates this by presenting parallel imagery from mythology, legend, and folklore. General amplification establishes the collective context of the dream and enables it to be seen as referring not only to a personal psychic problem but also to a general, collective problem common to all human experience. General amplification introduces one to the collective or archetypal psyche and at the same time helps the process of disidentifying the ego from the archetypal psyche.

Poetry and imaginative literature have always used amplification and analogy to suggest depths of meaning that would otherwise be missed. However, *Moby-Dick* is a particularly fine and far-reaching example of the amplification process. The entire book can be seen as an elaborate amplification of the psychological meaning of the whale and whale hunting. Since this is the case, it will be obviously impossible to circumscribe the meaning of the whale in a brief descriptive account. Melville himself has forewarned us concerning the impossibility of painting the portrait of the whale. After reviewing the various attempts to capture the reality of the whale in pictures, all of which fail in some respects, he concludes:

> For all these reasons, then, any way you may look at it, you must needs conclude that the great Leviathan is that one creature in the world which must remain unpainted to the last. True, one portrait may hit the mark much nearer than another, but none can hit it with any very considerable degree of exactness. So there is no earthly way of finding out precisely what the whale really looks like. And the only mode in which you can derive even a tolerable idea of his living contour, is by going whaling yourself; but by doing so, you run no small risk of being eternally stove and sunk by him. Wherefore, it seems to me you had best not be too fastidious in your curiosity touching this Leviathan. (Chapter 55)

Melville gives us the same warning when he talks about the dangers of the sea, the whales' habitat. He catalogs the terrors of the sea and continues:

> Consider the subtleness of the sea; how its most dreaded creatures glide under water, unapparent for the most part, and treacherously hidden beneath the loveliest tints of azure. Consider also the devilish brilliance and beauty of many of its most remorseless tribes, as the dainty embellished shape of many species of sharks. Consider, once more, the universal cannibalism of the sea; all whose creatures prey upon each other, carrying on eternal war since the world began.

Consider all this; and then turn to this green, gentle, and most docile earth; consider them both, the sea and the land; and do you not find a strange analogy to something in yourself? For as this appalling ocean surrounds the verdant land, so in the soul of man there lies one insular Tahiti, full of peace and joy, but encompassed by all the horrors of the half known life. God keep thee! Push not off from that isle, thou canst never return! (Chapter 58)

Here we have the compensatory opposite to Bulkington's attitude, "in landlessness alone resides the highest truth" (Chapter 23). The sea and the whale convey the same terrors and evoke the same warnings because they are different images to symbolize the same psychological fact. We do indeed find a "strange analogy" to something inside ourselves. The sea and the whale represent the primordial unconscious psyche which contains the aboriginal energies of life—numinous, awesome, and terrible. The sea is the collective unconscious and the whales that inhabit it are its major contents, the archetypes. The green island surrounded by the sea is the ego, the structural order of consciousness. Although an encounter with whales is dangerous, threatening drowning or dissolution of the conscious personality (psychosis), for the whaleman, the hero, whales are a vitally necessary source of energy to light the lamps of civilization. They must be hunted out, killed, and dismembered so that their raw natural energies can be transformed and applied to the uses of civilization—the purposes of the conscious discriminating personality. The whaling industry is thus a paradigm of the heroic effort of human consciousness to confront and transform the raw and aboriginal energies of the psyche.

The life of the whale hunters has many similarities to primitive hunting societies, and something of the same psychology applies to both. A primitive hunting group tends to have one animal on which it relies for sustenance, and its attitude toward this animal is a reverent one. This was true, for instance, of the Blackfoot Indians and the buffalo. The buffalo hunt is surrounded with sacred rite and ceremonial. Campbell writes: "Where the animal rites are properly celebrated by the people, there is a magical, wonderful accord between the beasts and those who have to hunt them. The buffalo dance properly performed insures that the creatures slaughtered shall be giving only their bodies, not their essence. . . . The hunt itself, therefore, is a rite of sacrifice, sacred and not a rawly secular affair."[1]

It was considered safe to kill particular buffaloes only if the reverent relation to the "great buffalo" is maintained. The "great buffalo" is the prototypical or essential animal; the eternal form or Platonic Idea of the species. "He is a figure of one more dimension than the others of his herd; timeless and indestructible. . . . He is a manifestation of that point, principle, or aspect of the realm of essence from which the creatures of his species spring."[2]

These considerations fit quite closely the hunting of whales in *Moby-Dick*. The whale hunters must kill whales for their own livelihood. But among all the whales in the ocean there is one special white whale, the "great" whale who will not permit himself to be captured. As with the "great Buffalo" of the Blackfoot who is timeless and indestructible, Moby-Dick was thought to be ubiquitous and immortal. He was the collective whale soul, the essential, eternal whale of which all other whales are only ephemeral manifestations. The sacred, special character of Moby-Dick is indicated by his whiteness. White or albino animals are typically considered sacred. Melville notes this fact, giving as examples the sacred white elephant of the Orient and the sacred white dog of the Iroquois.

To hunt the sacred white whale in the same way as all other whales are hunted is a sacrilege, a blasphemy, as Starbuck said. It represents a denial of the primitive hunter's religious attitude toward his victim. An assault on Moby-Dick is an assault on the very concept of the sacred. Now we begin to glimpse one of the fundamental meanings of Ahab's vengeful quest. It symbolizes the psychic dynamism which is responsible for the radical secularization of the modern industrial world. The very notion of the sacred, the numinous, the suprapersonal as a concept or category of experience is being extirpated from modern consciousness. Whales are the primitive, undifferentiated energies of nature; and, as one Melvillian commentator has put it, the whaleship is a machine for the exploitation of nature.[3] But if that exploitation process is turned against the sacred

---

[1] Joseph Campbell, *The Masks of God: Primitive Mythology* (New York: Viking Press, 1959), p. 293.

[2] Ibid., p. 292.

[3] "So if you want to know why Melville nailed us in *Moby-Dick*, consider whaling. Consider whaling as FRONTIER and INDUSTRY. A product

and suprapersonal aspect of man's own inner nature, she will turn against man and destroy him. The primitive attitude is right. When a primitive kills an animal for food or threshes his grain to make bread, he realizes he is sacrificing an aspect of deity. He therefore does it solemnly and religiously. His myths tell him that the animal or vegetation god is willing to offer himself freely as a sacrifice to the needs of men. But if this god-killing is done irreverently, with hybris, the god can turn against man and destroy him by withholding future food.

This may not be good logic for efficient hunting or agriculture, but it is sound psychology. The primitive attitude of natural piety may be considered superstitious and misplaced when applied to the external world; however, it is instinctive wisdom when applied to the inner psychic world. We all contain within us raw, undifferentiated natural life energies. If we are to have a conscious psychic life, it must feed on and transform these elemental energies. The archetypal energy-forms of the collective unconscious must be dismembered and broken down into assimilable units, like Osiris and like a captured whale, if the primordial energies are to be made available for conscious purposes. However, these are suprapersonal energies most aptly described as deities. Hence they must be approached with a religious attitude. Failure to do so is an act of hybris which does not recognize the existence of any power other than the will of the ego. In such a case the ego does not succeed in assimilating the energies of the archetypal form; rather, the archetype assimilates the ego. This is a disaster for the conscious personality. It undergoes a regression and lives out unconsciously the fate of the particular mythological image with which it is identified. And so it was with Ahab.

There can be no doubt that the white whale symbolizes the deity. A definite effort is made to assimilate the god-images of many of the world's mythologies to Moby-Dick. Let us pass some of the evidence in quick review.

Moby-Dick is called a "Job's whale" (Chapter 41), referring to Leviathan in the book of Job, one of the manifestations of Yahweh. The whale is remarked to be one of the incarnations of Vishnu in

wanted, men got it: big business. The Pacific as sweatshop. Men, led, against the biggest, damnedest creature nature uncorks. The whaleship as factory, the whaleboat the precision instrument." Charles Olson, *op. cit.*, p. 23.

the Matse Avatar (Chapter 55). The mad sailor, Gabriel, pronounced the white whale to be the Shaker God incarnated, and he prophesied "speedy doom to the sacrilegious assailants of his divinity" (Chapter 71). When Moby-Dick is first sighted, he is associated with Jupiter. "A gentle joyousness—a mighty mildness of repose in swiftness, invested the gliding whale. Not the white bull Jupiter swimming away with ravished Europa clinging to his graceful horns; his lovely, leering eyes sideways intent upon the maid; with smooth bewitching fleetness, rippling straight for the nuptial bower in Crete; not Jove, not that great majesty Supreme! did surpass the glorified White Whale as he so divinely swam" (Chapter 133). Later, Moby-Dick is called a "grand god": "warningly waving his bannered flukes in the air, the grand god revealed himself, sounded and went out of sight" (Chapter 133).

Much earlier, Ahab had described Moby-Dick as representing the transcendental reality behind the appearance of things. And such transcendental reality is another name for God. "All visible objects, man, are but as pasteboard masks. But in each event—in the living act, the undoubted deed—there, some unknown but still reasoning thing puts forth the mouldings of its features from behind the unreasoning mask. If man will strike, strike through the mask! How can the prisoner reach outside except by thrusting through the wall? To me, the white whale is that wall, shoved near to me." (Chapter 36)

Jung has demonstrated that the various representations of the god-image are expressions of the central archetype of the psyche, what he terms the Self. We must thus conclude that Moby-Dick is a symbol of the Self. One of the features of the phenomenology of the Self is that it is a paradoxical union of opposites. This theme appears in the discussion of the whale's vision. It is stated that the eyes of a whale are located in the sides of his head, and hence they look in opposite directions.

> A curious and most puzzling question might be started concerning this visual matter as touching the Leviathan. But I must be content with a hint. So long as a man's eyes are open in the light, the act of seeing is involuntary; that is, he cannot then help mechanically seeing whatever objects are before him. Nevertheless, any one's experience will teach him, that though he can take in an indiscriminating sweep of things at one glance, it is impossible for him, attentively, and completely, to

examine any two things—however large or however small—at one and the same instant of time; never mind if they lie side by side and touch each other. But if you now come to separate these two objects, and surround each by a circle of profound darkness; then in order to see one of them, in such a manner as to bring your mind to bear on it, the other will be utterly excluded from your contemporary consciousness. How is it, then, with the whale? True, both his eyes, in themselves must simultaneously act; but is his brain so much more comprehensive, combining, and subtle than man's, that he can at the same moment of time attentively examine two distinct prospects, one on one side of him, and the other in an exactly opposite direction? (Chapter 74)

The whale can relate to opposites simultaneously and thus transcend or reconcile them. This is one of the features of the Self which distinguishes it most clearly from that lesser center of personality, the conscious ego. Consciousness by its very nature exists by the separation of opposites by acquiring unilateral vision. The Self, the suprapersonal center of the personality has bilateral vision—it incorporates both sides of a pair of opposites in the total view and hence conveys wholeness.

The paradoxical nature of Moby-Dick is considered more extensively in regard to its color symbolism. A long chapter is devoted to discussing the significance of the whiteness of the whale. Although Melville records many of the positive and sacred associations to the color white, they are mentioned only to be discarded. For Melville, whiteness is equated with evil. The conventional meaning of the symbolic antithesis between black and white is reversed. We are told in effect that white is black—an enantiodromia is announced.

A woman once dreamt of Melville's white whale connected with a black whale "very much in the fashion of the Chinese T'ai-chi-t'u." The white whale had a black eye and the black whale a white eye.[4] ☯
For this dreamer, and likewise for Melville, the white whale Moby-Dick poses the archetypal problem of opposites. The Chinese T'ai-chi-t'u symbolizes the reciprocal relationship between two opposing principles. The white fish is Yang, the masculine principle of light, heaven, spirit, action. The black fish is Yin, the feminine

[4] Harriet A. Todd, *The Quest in the Works of Herman Melville* (privately printed, 1961), preface.

principle of darkness, earth, matter, receptivity. According to the Chinese notion, these two primal modes of being are in an alternating relation to one another, each containing the seed of its own opposite.

Moby-Dick is both black and white. It is white so far as its color is concerned. But it is symbolically black in its essential nature. Hence, it is a union of opposites. It is both Yang and Yin. It symbolizes paradoxically both the masculine principle of the father archetype and the feminine principle of the mother archetype. Its whiteness relates it to Yang, the spiritual logos principle and the father archetype, but its womblike, devouring aspects relate it to the mother archetype. I shall discuss these each in turn.

10 THE WHITENESS OF THE WHALE

MELVILLE RELATES the whiteness of the whale to spirituality when he says that whiteness is "the most meaning symbol of spiritual things, nay, the very veil of the Christian's Deity" (Chapter 42). The awfulness of the infinite, indefinite, disembodied, masculine spirit which is unrelated to the earthy, material, particularities of the Yin principle or mother archetype is described in the following passage on the horror of the color white:

> Is it that by its indefiniteness it shadows forth the heartless voids and immensities of the universe, and thus stabs us from behind with the thought of annihilation, when beholding the white depths of the milky way? Or is it, that as an essence whiteness is not so much a color as the visible absence of color, and at the same time the concrete of all colors; is it for these reasons that there is such a dumb blankness, full of meaning, in a wide landscape of snows—a colorless, all-color of atheism from which we shrink? And when we consider that other theory of the natural philosophers, that all other earthly hues—every stately or lovely emblazoning—the sweet tinges of sunset skies and woods; yea, and the gilded velvets of butterflies, and the butterfly cheeks of young girls; all these are but subtle deceits, not actually inherent in substances but only laid on from without; so that all deified Nature absolutely paints like the harlot, whose allurements cover nothing but the charnel house within; and when we proceed further,

and consider that the mystical cosmetic which produces every one of her hues, the great principle of light, for ever remains white or colorless in itself, and if operating without medium upon matter, would touch all objects, even tulips and roses, with its own blank tinge—pondering all this, the palsied universe lies before us a leper; and like wilful travellers in Lapland, who refuse to wear colored and coloring glasses upon their eyes, so the wretched infidel gazes himself blind at the monumental white shroud that wraps all the prospect around him. And of all these things, the Albino Whale was the symbol. Wonder ye then at the fiery hunt? (Chapter 42)

Whiteness is described as symbolizing the impersonal, infinite, eternal undefined vastness that lies behind the personal, particular, concrete, and ordinary phenomena of everyday life. It is the original undifferentiated whole before it has been refracted—dismembered as it were—into its particular component parts. It is the infinite and impersonal that has never been subjected to the personalizing process, that is, the process which incarnates the eternal forms in personal, particular manifestations and images. The eternal forms of the spirit or masculine principle make themselves manifest by embodiment in particular, material incarnations. The matter or matrix of these embodiments pertain to the Yin principle or mother archetype. Matter and matrix are cognate with *mater*, mother. If the spirit remains completely disembodied with no personal, temporal, material expression or imagery, it becomes a blinding horror, wholly transcendent, that provides no personal, particular, immanent aspect by which to relate to it.

Shelley uses the same image in a more innocent, romantic way,

> The One remains, the many change and pass,
> Heaven's light forever shines, Earth's shadows fly;
> Life, like a dome of many-coloured glass,
> Stains the white radiance of Eternity.[5]

In the passage, Melville refers to certain eighteenth-century philosophical theories which state that the categories by which we perceive the particular manifestations of the outer world are subjective ones projected onto phenomena or, as Melville says, "laid on from without." There is no color or beauty in nature. The colors

[5] "Adonais," *Selected Prose and Poetry of Percy Bysshe Shelley*, Carlos Baker, ed. (New York: Modern Library, 1951), LII, ll. 460–63.

and qualities we appear to see are no more than the artifice of our own modes of perception and hence have no substantial reality. From the psychological viewpoint, this particular philosophical theory expresses the supremacy of two psychic functions, thinking and intuition, and the depreciation of the two other psychic functions, feeling and sensation. The personal value judgments of feeling and the reality, sensory perceptions of sensation are declared to have no valid basis—they are no more than deceitful illusions, nothing but subjective. Now, these two functions that the philosophers rejected are the same ones which we have already noted to be Melville's undeveloped functions. Feeling and sensation are the functions which relate the individual to the personal value and the specific, concrete aspects of his experience. They are the functions which serve the personalizing process and help the individual feel at home in the universe. They are the functions that mediate the Yin aspect of life. If they are ruled out of order or developmentally arrested, one is exposed without any protective buffer to the infinite, impersonal, unstructured immensity of pure, disembodied spirit.

A crucial aspect of early psychological development is what might be called the process of personalization or incarnation of the archetypal images. Initially, the emerging ego is directly exposed to the transports and terrors of the undifferentiated and unmediated power of the archetypes. However, with adequate parental and other personal relationships, some of the raw transcendent energies are personalized and made immanent. The image of the archetypal father, for instance, cannot be endured in its transcendent, unstructured form (one cannot view the face of God and live). It must be mediated through a particular, concrete relationship with a person who can carry partial aspects of the archetype. It is for this reason that the child's relation to the parents is so vitally important to his subsequent psychic development. If the parents have not provided adequate human relationship for the child, they are not fulfilling their function to personalize and mediate the archetypal energies. In such a case, a kind of hole is left between the conscious personality and the collective unconscious. Through this hole can come dangerous eruptions of powerful unstructured energies. The extreme case of failure of the archetypes to become personalized is found in overt schizophrenia, where the ego is literally inundated by boundless, primordial images which have never been mediated or made immanent through human relationships or connection with concrete reality.

This vital need for the personalization of the archetype accounts for the way in which many patients cling obstinately to their original experience of the parents. If, for instance, there has been a largely negative, destructive, parental experience, the patient may find it very difficult to accept and endure a positive parent experience. A person will, for instance, persist in a negative orientation to the father archetype simply because that is the aspect of the image which has been concretized and personalized in his own life and therefore has an element of safety and security, even though it is negative. For such a person to encounter the positive side of the archetype is threatening because, since this side has never been personalized, it carries a transpersonal magnitude which threatens to dissolve the established boundaries of the ego. Emily Dickinson describes this state of affairs in these lines:

> I can wade grief,
> Whole pools of it,—
> I'm used to that.
> But the least push of joy
> Breaks up my feet,
> And I tip—drunken.
> Let no pebble smile,
> 'Twas the new liquor,—
> That was all![6]

Melville's relation to his father is an example of an inadequate personalization of an archetype. It left Melville exposed to the excessive, damaging power of the Spirit Father archetype, which like the whiteness of Lapland is blinding (amputating, castrating) when viewed directly without the mediation of an adequate relation to a personal father.[7]

When an archetype has not been adequately personalized or mediated in one's outer life experience, this defect can sometimes be

[6] *The Complete Poems of Emily Dickinson*, Thomas E. Johnson, ed. (Boston: Little, Brown & Co., 1960), no. 252, p. 115.

[7] The association of the whiteness of the whale with the personal father is verified by a passage from *Pierre* in which the father is referred to. as "the perfect marble form" of his departed father; without blemish, unclouded, snow-white, and serene." Melville, *Pierre*, Book IV, Chapter 1.

remedied by a process of inner mediation through the imagination. In Melville's description, whiteness is so devastating because it is infinite, without boundaries or specific characteristics. It has the same aspect as landlessness had for Bulkington, it is "shoreless, indefinite as God" (Chapter 23). The refraction process which breaks up infinite whiteness into particular manifestations to which the ego is capable of relating can be promoted by the image-making powers of the imagination. Here Ahab's significance as image-maker (idolator) is pertinent. Ahab's attack against the whiteness of Moby-Dick represents the heroic effort of the ego, through creative imagination, to refract and dismember the infinite, boundless transpersonal psychic energy by embodying it in specific images. Such images would then be able to mediate between the ego and the transpersonal psyche in the same way as Moses' brazen serpent operated for the Israelites in the wilderness.

The infinite whiteness of the whale is not described in neutral or balanced terms. The dark, evil side is predominant, and in several passages, Moby-Dick is described as the incarnation of evil. Melville's experience with his father involved the fearful encounter with insanity and death at the tender age of twelve. It is thus quite understandable that the father archetype should be seen largely in its frightful, demonic aspect. Hence, Moby-Dick is called "the gliding great demon of the seas of life" (Chapter 41), and it is remarked that "though in many of its aspects this visible world seems formed in love, the invisible spheres were formed in fright" (Chapter 42). Melville had a vision of radical evil. Although one-sided and conditioned by childhood trauma, it is none the less true. William James describes the same acute awareness of evil which contradicts the naïve attitude of healthy-mindedness:

> The normal process of life contains moments as bad as any of those which insane melancholy is filled with, moments in which radical evil gets its innings and takes its solid turn. The lunatic's visions of horror are all drawn from the material of daily fact. Our civilization is founded on the shambles, and every individual existence goes out in a lonely spasm of helpless agony. If you protest, my friend, wait till you arrive there yourself! To believe in the carnivorous reptiles of geologic times is hard for our imagination—they seem too much like mere museum specimens. Yet there is no tooth in anyone of those museum-skulls that did not daily through long years of the foretime

hold fast to the body struggling in despair of some fated living victim. Forms of horror just as dreadful to the victims, if on a smaller spatial scale, fill the world about us today. Here on our very hearths and in our gardens the infernal cat plays with the panting mouse, or holds the hot bird fluttering in her jaws. Crocodiles and rattlesnakes and pythons are at this moment vessels of life as real as we are; their loathesome existence fills every minute of every day that drags its length along; and whenever they or other wild beasts clutch their living prey, the deadly horror which an agitated melancholic feels is the literally right reaction on the situation.[8]

Robert Frost, in his poem "Design," describes a similar vision of evil, associated, like Moby-Dick, with the color white:

> I found a dimpled spider, fat and white,
> On a white heal-all, holding up a moth
> Like a white piece of rigid satin cloth—
> Assorted characters of death and blight
> Mixed ready to begin the morning right,
> Like the ingredients of a witches' broth—
> A snow-deep spider, a flower like a froth,
> And dead wings carried like a paper kite.
> What had the flower to do with being white,
> The wayside blue and innocent heal-all?
> What brought the kindred spider to that height,
> Then steered the white moth thither in the night?
> What but design of darkness to appall?—
> If design govern in a thing so small.[9]

The acute, tortured awareness of radical evil as an aspect of God is a theme that runs through all of *Moby-Dick* and indeed through almost all of Melville's subsequent writings. In Chapter 40, it is remarked on bitterly. A Negro sailor has been taunted by a white sailor because of the color of his skin. They are ready to fight, and the crew, lusting for blood, sadistically eggs them on. They call for a "ring, a ring." The Manx sailor replies, "Ready formed. There! The ringed horizon. In that ring Cain struck Abel. Sweet work, right work! No? Why then God, mad'st thou the ring?" Indeed,

[8] William James, *The Varieties of Religious Experience* (New York: Modern Library, 1936), pp. 160ff.
[9] *Complete Poems of Robert Frost* (New York: Holt, Rinehart and Winston, 1962), p. 396.

the invisible spheres were formed in fright and by God himself. The whiteness of the Christian God of Love is a deceit that only covers the "charnel house within."

Melville, at the age of thirty-two, is grappling with a fearful paradox. He was exposed precociously to the harsh reality of the dark side of life. Not that this experience is rare. It is still, tragically, much too frequent. But Melville was gifted with the expressive and image-making powers which could give his soul-searing dilemma living form in *Moby-Dick*.

When evil is felt to be intolerable, when consciousness is unable to relate it meaningfully to life, some outlet must be found. The resentment accumulates which must have some object. In such a case, a scapegoat mechanism is likely to take over. Thus it was with Ahab. The white whale became for him a kind of divine scapegoat. This is described in a magnificent passage in Chapter 41:

> The White Whale swam before him as the monomaniac incarnation of all those malicious agencies which some deep men feel eating in them, till they are left living on with half a heart and half a lung. That intangible malignity which has been from the beginning; to whose dominion even the modern Christians ascribe one-half of the worlds; which the ancient Ophites of the east reverenced in their statute devil;—Ahab did not fall down and worship it like them; but deliriously transferring its idea to the abhorred White Whale, he pitted himself, all mutilated, against it. All that most maddens and torments; all that stirs up the lees of things; all truth with malice in it; all that cracks the sinews and cakes the brain; all the subtle demonisms of life and thought; all evil, to crazy Ahab, were visibly personified, and made practically assailable in Moby Dick. He piled upon the whale's white hump the sum of all the general rage and hate felt by his whole race from Adam down; and then, as if his chest had been a mortar, he burst his hot heart's shell upon it.

For those who don't believe in evil as something innate and fundamental, for those who would interpret Melville's preoccupation with evil to be solely a consequence of his personal life trauma, he gives an example from the animal world of the pre-existent, archetypal knowledge of evil.

> Tell me, why this strong young colt, foaled in some peaceful valley of Vermont, far removed from all beasts of prey—why is it that upon the sunniest day, if you but shake a fresh buffalo robe behind him, so that

he cannot even see it but only smells its wild animal mustiness—why will he start, snort, and with bursting eyes paw the ground in phrensies of affright? There is no remembrance in him of any gorings of wild creatures in his green northern home, so that the strange mustiness he smells cannot recall to him anything associated with the experience of former perils; for what knows he, this New England colt, of the black bisons of distant Oregon?

No: but here thou beholdest even in a dumb brute the instinct of the knowledge of the demonism in the world. Though thousands of miles from Oregon, still when he smells that savage musk, the rending, goring bison herds are as present as to the deserted wild foal of the prairies, which this instant they may be trampling into dust. . . . Though neither knows where lie the nameless things of which the mystic sign gives forth such hints; yet with me as with the colt, somewhere those things must exist. (Chapter 42)

In this brilliant passage, Melville demonstrates that he has discovered and consciously understood the nature of the collective unconscious. A century later, Jung was to make the same analogy between the archetypes, the a priori experience-forms of the psyche, and the innate instinctive behavior patterns in animals.

Instinct and the archaic mode of archetypal images meet in the biological conception of the "pattern of behavior." There are in fact no amorphous instincts, as every instinct bears in itself the pattern of its situation. Always it fulfills an image, and the image has fixed qualities. . . . Such an image is an *a priori* type, i.e., an archetype. . . . We may say that the image represents the meaning of the instinct.[10]

Other passages also express Melville's experience of the collective unconscious. In Chapter 41 we read: "Winding far down from within the very heart of this spiked Hotel de Cluny where we here stand—however grand and wonderful, now quit it;—and take your way, ye nobler, sadder souls, to those vast Roman halls of Thermes; where far beneath the fantastic towers of men's upper earth, his root of grandeur, his whole awful essence sits in bearded state; an antique buried beneath antiquities, and throned on torsoes! So with a broken throne, the great gods mock that captive king; so like a Caryatid, he patient sits, upholding on his frozen brow the piled entablatures of ages. Wind ye down there, ye prouder, sadder souls! question

[10] C. G. Jung, *The Structure and Dynamics of the Psyche*, CW 8 (Princeton, N.J.: Princeton University Press, 1970), par. 398.

that proud, sad king! A family likeness! aye, he did beget ye, ye young exiled royalties; and from your grim sire only will the old State-secret come."

The Hotel de Cluny referred to was a museum in Paris which Melville had visited. The building had been built about 1490 on the ruins of an old Roman palace, and it was claimed that this palace itself had been built on still earlier ruins. Hence, the Hotel de Cluny becomes an apt symbol for the human psyche which contains in its lower, unconscious layers archaic remnants of man's collective racial history. Melville's image of the Hotel de Cluny is paralleled by a dream of Jung's which he had shortly prior to his development of the theory of the collective unconscious.

> I was in a house I did not know, which had two stories. It was "my house." I found myself in the upper story, where there was a kind of salon furnished with fine old pieces in rococo style. On the walls hung a number of precious old paintings. I wondered that this should be my house, and thought, "not bad." But then it occurred to me that I did not know what the lower floor looked like. Descending the stairs, I reached the ground floor. There everything was much older, and I realized that this part of the house must date from about the fifteenth or sixteenth century. The furnishings were medieval; the floors were of red brick. Everywhere it was rather dark. I went from one room to another, thinking, "Now I really must explore the whole house." I came upon a heavy door, and opened it. Beyond it, I discovered a stone stairway that led down into the cellar. Descending again, I found myself in a beautifully vaulted room which looked exceedingly ancient. . . . I knew that the walls dated from Roman times. My interest by now was intense. I looked more closely at the floor. It was of stone slabs, and in one of these I discovered a ring. When I pulled it, the stone slab lifted, and again I saw a stairway of narrow stone steps leading down into the depths. These too I descended, and entered a low cave cut into the rock. Thick dust lay on the floor, and in the dust were scattered bones and broken pottery, like remains of a primitive culture. I discovered two human skulls, obviously very old and half disintegrated. Then I awoke.[11]

Melville's passage about the Hotel de Cluny as well as the previous one describing the New England colt has a definite, negative cast. They both emphasize the dark and the evil side of the psychic

---

[11] Jung, *Memories, Dreams, Reflections,* pp. 158–59.

depths. The image of the sad, bearded patriarchal king sitting on a broken throne indicates the deep-seated damage that had been done to the archetypal father. Melville unquestionably plumbed the collective unconscious to a considerable depth. However, because of his particular personal life experience, it carried a darker and more negative aspect than it might for someone else. Melville might say with Ahab, "So far gone am I in the dark side of earth, that its other side, the theoretic bright one, seems but uncertain twilight to me." (Chapter 127)

11 THE WHALE AS SPHINX AND MEDUSA

THE WHITE WHALE carries in its paradoxical symbolism not only the masculine, spiritual Yang principle of the father archetype but also the manifold meanings of the mother archetype. This is indicated by the association of the whale to that enigmatic feminine monster, the Sphinx. In Chapter 70, entitled "The Sphynx," Ahab gives a soliloquy while gazing at the mammoth decapitated head of a captured whale:

> It was a black and hooded head; and hanging there in the midst of so intense a calm, it seemed the Sphinx's in the desert. "Speak, thou vast and venerable head," muttered Ahab, "which, though ungarnished with a beard, yet here and there lookest hoary with mosses; speak, mighty head, and tell us the secret thing that is in thee. Of all divers, thou hast dived the deepest. That head upon which the upper sun now gleams, has moved amid this world's foundations. Where unrecorded names and navies rust, and untold hopes and anchors rot; where in her murderous hold this frigate earth is ballasted with bones of millions of the drowned; there, in that awful waterland, there was thy most familiar home. . . . O head! thou has seen enough to split the planets and make an infidel of Abraham, and not one syllable is thine!" (Chapter 70)

The whale head was associated with the Sphinx, which brings us to the symbolism of that mythical creature. The name means "throttler," reminding us that Ahab dies in his encounter with Moby-Dick by being throttled by his own harpoon line. The Sphinx had the head of a woman and the body of a lion, indicating that it belongs largely to the animal world of instinct which has not yet been humanized by consciousness. It was said to be a guardian of the underworld. In the Oedipus myth, the Sphinx was a characteristic devouring feminine monster who posed riddles and then devoured those who could not answer them. The Sphinx thus represents the inviolable mystery of life. The tragedy of Oedipus began with his apparently effortless answer to the riddle of the Sphinx. Jung's comment on Oedipus' relation to the Sphinx is pertinent here:

> Oedipus, thinking he had overcome the Sphinx sent by the mother-goddess merely because he had solved her childishly simple riddle, fell a victim to matriarchal incest and had to marry Jocasta, his mother. . . . This had all those tragic consequences which could easily have been avoided if only Oedipus had been sufficiently intimidated by the frightening appearance of the "terrible" or "devouring" mother whom the Sphinx personified. . . . Little did he know that the riddle of the Sphinx can never be solved merely by the wit of man. . . . The riddle was, in fact, the trap which the Sphinx laid for the unwary wanderer. Over-estimating his intellect in a typically masculine way, Oedipus walked right into it, and all unknowingly committed the crime of incest.[1]

Ahab, like Oedipus, was undone by his failure to experience appropriate fear in relation to the whale. We are reminded of Pip's prayer, "Oh, thou big white God aloft there somewhere in yon darkness, have mercy on this small black boy down here; preserve him from all men that have no bowels to feel fear!" (Chapter 40)

Ahab, while paying lip service to the secret knowledge of the whale, reveals none the less his presumption that this knowledge is no secret to him when he says, "O head! thou has seen enough to split the planets and make an infidel of Abraham." How does Ahab know that the whale's knowledge is destructive—would split planets and destroy faith? Ahab thinks he knows the secret of life. Like Oedipus, he thinks he has answered the riddle. This is his fatal hybris that must lead inevitably to his downfall. As the proverb puts it, the fear of God is the beginning of wisdom. Ahab has repressed all his fear, his capacity for wonder and awe. He thinks he has discovered the nature of the deity—thinks it to be no more than destructive malice toward man. In fact, however, he is only seeing the reflected image of himself.

[1] Jung, *Symbols of Transformation,* par. 264ff.

This conversation with a head has a parallel in an ancient practice of consulting an oracle head. Cleomenes of Sparta is said to have had the head of his friend Archonides preserved in a jar of honey which he then consulted as an oracle. The same was said of Orpheus' head.[2] It has been suggested that the teraphim of the Old Testament Israelites, which were used as oracles, may have been mummified heads. According to legend, in a collection of midrashim from the twelfth century:

> The teraphim were idols, and they were made in the following way. The head of a man, who had to be a first-born, was cut off and the hair plucked out. The head was then sprinkled with salt and annointed with oil. Afterwards a little plaque, of copper or gold, was inscribed with the name of an idol and placed under the tongue of the decapitated head. The head was set up in a room, candles were lit before it, and the people made obeisance. And if any man fell down before it, the head began to speak, and answered all questions that were addressed to it.[3]

The "head oracle" may have been the archaic origin of that conventional, dramatic device, the soliloquy to the skull, e.g., as in *Hamlet*. The skull or decapitated head can represent one who has passed over into the other world, i.e., the unconscious, and is asked to report on things from that broader perspective. Or, alternatively, the head, being the seat of the psyche and being round, signifying wholeness, can symbolize the psyche in its totality. R. B. Onians writes regarding head symbolism in antiquity:

> There is this various evidence that the head was holy with potency by which to swear and make appeal and was thought to contain the life or psyche. . . . It had nothing to do with ordinary consciousness (perception, thought and feeling being the business of the chest and its organs), but instead was the vehicle of life itself, of that which continues and does not die.[4]

Thus, the head would signify the archetypal psyche, and to consult it as an oracle would mean to consult the "eternal wisdom" of the unconscious.

[2] C. G. Jung, *Psychology and Religion: West and East*, CW 11 (Princeton, N.J.: Princeton University Press, 1970), par. 373.
[3] Cited by Jung, Ibid., par. 368.
[4] R. B. Onians, *The Origins of European Thought* (Cambridge: Cambridge University Press, 1951), p. 108.

Without his realizing it, Ahab received an answer from the whale-head oracle. His soliloquy to the head is interrupted by a cry from the masthead that a ship was bearing down on them. Ahab's reaction indicates he dimly sensed that the ship's sudden appearance had a deeper meaning.

> That lively cry upon this deadly calm might almost convert a better man. . . . Would now St. Paul would come along that way, and to my breezelessness bring his breeze! O nature and O soul of man! How far beyond all utterance are your linked analogies; not the smallest atom stirs or lives on matter, but has its cunning duplicate in mind. (Chapter 70)

The message the ship brought was first of all in its name, Jeroboam. The Biblical Jeroboam was a king of Israel, an earlier version of Ahab, who set up golden calves to be worshipped and encouraged the return to the Canaanite religion of Baal. He and his house were destroyed by Yahweh. On the ship Jeroboam, a plague had broken out, symbolizing the psychic infection that existed on Ahab's ship. Also on the Jeroboam was a crazy prophet, Gabriel, who, when he heard that Ahab was hunting Moby-Dick, warned him wildly to "Beware of the blasphemer's end." This, then, was the response of the oracle head. But it went unnoticed by Ahab.

Another set of associations connect the whale with another mother-monster, Medusa, the Gorgon slain by Perseus. When Ahab first made his appearance on deck, the initial image used to describe him was that he looked like "Cellini's cast Perseus" (Chapter 28). Later Starbuck says, "Oh, God! to sail with such a heathen crew that have small touch of human mothers in them. Whelped somewhere by the sharkish sea. The white whale is their demigorgon" (Chapter 38). Finally it is stated (Chapter 82) that "the gallant Perseus, a son of Jupiter, was the first whaleman."

What then is the story of the first whaleman, Perseus? Perseus had no father. His mother, Danae, conceived him by Zeus, who came to her in a shower of golden rain. Since his grandfather Acrisius had been told by an oracle that his grandson would kill him, he attempted to dispose of the infant Perseus and his mother by locking them in a wooden ark and casting it into the sea. However, the ark washed ashore on an island. Danae and Perseus were rescued by the fisherman, Dictys, and were accepted as guests in the house of Polydectes, king of the island. Perseus grew to manhood. Polydectes wished to marry Danae. In order to get rid of Perseus, who opposed the marriage, he tricked him into offering to bring him the head of Medusa. Medusa was a horrible monster who turned to stone anyone that looked at her. With the help of Athena and Hermes, Perseus attacked Medusa. He avoided the fatal consequences of looking on Medusa directly by seeing her in the reflection of a polished shield provided by Athena. With a sword provided by Hermes, he cut off Medusa's head. At once, from the decapitated body of Medusa the winged horse Pegasus emerged and flew into the sky. On his homeward trip, he spied a naked woman chained to a cliff on the coast of Joffa. This was Andromeda, daughter of Cepheus and Cassiopeia. Andromeda was being offered as a sacrificial victim to a sea monster in punishment for Cassiopeia's arrogance in claiming to be more beautiful than the sea nymphs. Perseus rescued her by killing the sea monster, married her, and returned to his home. Wicked Polydectes was destroyed by being shown Medusa's head, and eventually Perseus took over the kingdom of his grandfather Acrisius.

Perseus, in common with almost all heroes, has a supernatural conception and immediately after birth is treated with hostility by the established authorities. The hero represents the principle of consciousness and transformation. Its divine parentage indicates that this urge derives from the transpersonal levels of the psyche. The established powers of the *status quo* are invariably hostile to its birth because it presages the death or transformation of the old order. Thus, Acrisius is told by the oracle that he will be killed by his grandson. Each generation and what it stands for must be killed by the generations that immediately follow. This is necessary and proper if life is to be perpetually renewed. The infant hero survives the efforts of the established authorities to destroy him because he is divinely sanctioned. Hence, Perseus survived his abandonment to the sea, was washed ashore, and reached manhood. Then he is exposed to the hostility of another father figure who expects to get rid of him by sending him off on an impossible task. This apparently hostile act, however, proves to be just the challenge needed to evoke and realize the hero's latent capacities.

Perseus goes off to do battle with the dangerous female monster, Medusa, who represents the destructive aspect of the Great Mother archetype. Her most dangerous feature is her ability to turn to stone all men who look at her. This refers to the paralyzing or congealing effect that the Great Mother can have on the emotional life of a man. A man once dreamed that he was gazing at a bitter old woman. As he watched her, he became paralyzed, unable to move or speak. Here is a modern version of the Greek Medusa, showing that these ancient myths are still very much alive.

In a larger sense, Medusa represents the horror of material exist-ence (matter = *mater*), which cannot be endured if gazed upon di-rectly. Ahab had seen Medusa directly in his previous encounter with Moby-Dick, and the sight had turned him to stone. His emo-tional life was petrified into a single obsession. Did not Stubb dream of Ahab as a stony pyramid? Using Melville's own image, "like wil-ful travellers in Lapland, who refuse to wear colored glasses upon their eyes," Ahab gazed himself blind. Ahab's resentment and venge-ful attitude are symptoms of his emotional paralysis and petrifaction. It is no accident that there is not a single significant feminine figure in Moby-Dick. The anima (Andromeda) has not yet been separated from the feminine monster; only Medusa exists, and the encounter with her has been a failure. One more potential hero has been turned to stone.

The outcome of Perseus' efforts is different. He does not rely on his own efforts alone but seeks the assistance of the gods. Hermes provides him with a sword, in the language of whalemen, a special harpoon. From Athena, he gets a polished shield and careful instruc-tions on how to use it as a mirror so that the paralyzing view of Me-dusa can be approached indirectly, by reflection, and hence safely. This symbolic image of the mirror is most interesting. There is surely good reason for our using the image of the reflective capacity of a mirror in describing the reflective capacity of consciousness. To reflect means to bend or throw back. We can see what is behind us only by means of a mirror. A mirror thus symbolizes the capacity to see the nature of our unconscious motivations——that which lies be-hind or in back of consciousness. The capacity for reflection is the ability to question our naïve and immediate reactions to things. We are also provided a reflecting mirror by which to get a view of our unconscious selves through the reactions of others. Ahab neglected both of these opportunities for reflection. He gave no inner reflec-tion to the motives of his chase, and he utterly disregarded the reac-tions of others, such as Starbuck, who could have provided him a reflective mirror by which to see the nature of his own unconscious drives.

There is also another aspect to the reflected image. Not only does it reverse the direction of light rays, enabling us to see what is behind us, but also, and this is what is emphasized in the Perseus myth, it softens or mitigates the effects of the raw, elemental experience. Although it is damaging to look at the raw phenomenon, it is safe or bearable to view it through the mediation of a reflected image. I am reminded of the warnings of the ophthalmologists before a solar eclipse. It causes blindness to look at the sun with the unprotected naked eye; one must either use a heavily smoked glass or else watch a reflected image. I have been told personally by a schizophrenic patient that during the height of his psychotic period he was able to gaze directly at the sun without hurting his eyes but that as he began to recover this became quite impossible. It is uncertain whether this was a fact or a fantasy. Either way, it indicates a state of being at one with the central source of energy (sun) during the psychotic experience.

Athena's mirror-shield is a symbol of the whole human acculturating process. Art, literature, ritual, drama, games, etc., all provide a mirror for existence in which the great world of being is reflected and mediated by a smaller world of experience, breaking up the totality of raw experience into assimilable units and promoting the process of transformation. So it happened with Medusa. From her decapitated body sprang the winged horse Pegasus, the beloved of the Muses—he who created their Hippocrene fountain of inspiration.

A winged horse symbolizes a process of libido transformation. A horse represents earthy animal instinctuality. A horse with wings would thus signify instinctual energy which has undergone a transformation—become spiritualized. A quantity of psychic energy which has been bound to the unconscious in the negative form of the monster Medusa has been released and becomes available for use by the conscious personality. This corresponds to the psychological meaning of whale hunting. When whales are captured, cut up, and processed, the energies their bodies contain are transformed. Instead of serving whale purposes they serve human purposes. The whale energy is wrested away from the automatisms of nature and applied to the uses of consciousness and civilization. Like the houses, parks, and gardens of New Bedford, the energies that operate civilized consciousness are "harpooned and dragged up hither from the bottom of the sea." (Chapter 6)

Following his successful engagement with Medusa, Perseus encounters another monster. It is as though the fight with the monster must be repeated on another level of conscious awareness. On the first occasion, unknown to Perseus, Pegasus was imprisoned in Medusa, waiting for release. On the second, Andromeda is the prisoner of the sea monster and in need of rescue. Now, however, the anima is a separate entity existing independently of the monster, although still under its power. This indicates a definite development of consciousness. Andromeda, the anima, corresponding to man's capacity to love freely and maturely, has been partially freed from the mother monster, representing infantile maternal dependence. This phase of the Perseus myth has no parallel in *Moby-Dick*. In the latter, the anima did not even reach existence as a personification separate from the monster. As previously noted, Ahab came to grief because he lacked a mirror.

Andromeda and the sea monster is only one example of the ubiquitous archetypal theme of the beautiful woman held prisoner by the beast and in need of rescue by the hero. The woman is the anima, the human soul which is a captive of the unregenerate instinctive forces in the psyche. Andromeda becomes the monster's victim because of Cassiopeia's arrogance. In fact, the monster will be the arrogant hybris itself. In the context of the whole story, this will mean that Perseus had an inflation following his success against Medusa which, as it were, reactivated the monster and obliged him to do battle with it again.

After Perseus' return home, the father figures Polydectes and Acrisius, representing the old order, are killed. Perseus takes over the kingdom of Acrisius, signifying that he has established his own independent relation to life. In *Moby-Dick*, this theme of "the death of the old king" would correspond to the end of the book when Ahab is killed, leaving Ishmael, the sole survivor, to be the carrier of consciousness.

Although Ahab failed in the role of Perseus against Medusa, Melville succeeded. His creative imagination (Athena) provided the mirror-shield, and he in turn, by writing *Moby-Dick*, has contributed a significant piece to that grand mosaic-mirror of human culture.

12 FEDALLAH, THE AVENGING ANGEL

UNKNOWN to the others, Ahab had secretly brought on board the Pequod his own whaleboat crew with its leader, Fedallah. When whales were first sighted and the boats were being lowered, these strange stowaways suddenly make their appearance. "With a start all glared at dark Ahab, who was surrounded by five dusky phantoms that seemed fresh formed out of air." (Chapter 47) Fedallah, their leader, was the most striking one. His figure "was tall and swart, with one white tooth evilly protruding from its steel-like lips. A rumpled Chinese jacket of black cotton funereally invested him, with wide black trousers of the same dark stuff. But strangely crowning this ebonness was a glistening white plaited turban" (Chapter 48).

Fedallah is clearly related to the devil; if he is not the devil himself, at least he is one of his subordinates. His companions are described as "a race notorious for a certain diabolism of subtilty, and by some honest white mariners supposed to be the paid spies and secret confidential agents on the water of the devil." (Chapter 48) Stubb says, "I take that Fedallah to be the devil in disguise." (Chapter 73) Although it is not described with the same clarity, it is evident that Ahab's relation to Fedallah has a certain infernal parallel to Ishmael's relation to Queequeg. Just as Ishmael concluded a pact of eternal friendship with Queequeg which had its external symbol in the monkey rope that connected them, so Ahab was in some way bound to Fedallah. "By what sort of unaccountable tie he soon evinced himself to be linked with Ahab's peculiar fortunes; nay, so far as to have some sort of a half-hinted influence; Heaven knows, but it might have been even authority over him." (Chapter 50)

In addition, Fedallah carried for Ahab something of the same characteristics of primal natural man and original wholeness as did Queequeg for Ishmael. Fedallah

> was such a creature as civilized, domestic people in the temperate zone only see in their dreams, and that but dimly; but the like of whom now and then glide among the unchanging Asiatic communities, es-

pecially the Oriental isles to the east of the continent—those insulated, immemorial, unalterable countries, which even in these modern days still preserve much of the ghostly aboriginalness of earth's primal generations, when the memory of the first man was a distinct recollection, and all men his descendants, unknowing whence he came, eyed each other as real phantoms, and asked of the sun and the moon why they were created and to what end. (Chapter 50)

Just as Queequeg revealed his relation to the original wholeness of the primordial Self by his square tatoos and his mark, a Maltese cross, so Fedallah's similar meaning is indicated by his being associated with the "primal generations" and the "first-man." The image of the primal man, the Anthropos, has been extensively described by Jung.[5] It is a symbol of the Self, the integrated, whole man. Totality and the union of opposites is also implied by Fedallah's clothes, which combine the opposite colors, black and white. Queequeg and Fedallah being part-personalities rooted in the unconscious, both carry intimations of the primal wholeness. They are the shadows respectively of Ishmael and Ahab. This is specifically stated at one point. "And Ahab chanced so to stand, that the Parsee occupied his shadow; while, if the Parsee's shadow was there at all it seemed only to blend with and lengthen Ahab's." (Chapter 73)

Having noted the correspondences between Queequeg and Fedallah, we must also mention the differences. In a sense they are a pair of opposites paralleling the opposite natures of their corresponding partners, Ishmael and Ahab. Queequeg is largely a positive figure embodying strengths and fortitudes that complement the weakness of Ishmael. He represents the noble savage. Fedallah, on the other hand, is the diabolical savage. He conveys a sense of darkness and evil. He does not complement Ahab's conscious sense of heroic strength by weakness the way Queequeg's strength complements Ishmael's weakness. That particular shadow function is reserved for Pip. However, Fedallah's evident moral inferiority does compensate Ahab's conscious sense of nobility, just as Queequeg's nobility compensates Ishmael's ignoble escapism. With the voyage well under way, we have, then, a pair of mutual assistance pacts, together making a quaternity. Ishmael is bound to Queequeg in mutual love, and Ahab is bound to Fedallah in their mutual quest for vengeance.

[5] C. G. Jung, *Mysterium Coniunctionis*, CW 14 (Princeton, N.J.: Princeton University Press, 1970), par. 544ff.; also *Psychology and Alchemy*, par. 456ff.

Another aspect of Fedallah's meaning is suggested by his name. The origins and implications of the name Fedallah have been most interestingly elaborated by Dorothee Finkelstein.[6] It is an Islamic name compounded of two elements: *feda*, meaning "sacrifice" or "ransom," and *Allah*, meaning "God." It thus means "the sacrifice of God." The cognate term *Fedai*, meaning "he who offers up his life," was applied to the medieval sect of Islamic mystics called Assassins. These were avenging ministers or destroying angels of God who were pledged to commit murder in the service of Allah. The word "assassin" derives from *hashish* or "hemp," the source of marijuana, and was applied to these religious killers because they consumed hashish in order to induce an ecstatic state of communion with the deity. These connections are most interesting in the light of Fedallah's prophecy to Ahab that "hemp only can kill thee." (Chapter 117) "The Fedais or assassins were sent to all parts of the world on missions of assassination as a religious duty. They were distinguished by the determination with which they exposed their lives in order to destroy their victims, the voyages which they undertook to achieve their purpose, and the calmness with which they waited for the moment favorable to their design."[7] Fedallah's name thus suggests that he is the avenging agent of God, Fate's assassin, sent to punish Ahab for hybris. The weapon of assassination is hemp or hashish, which causes intoxication and loss of reason.

Immediately following the appearance of Fedallah, a new phenomenon is encountered. The spirit spout appears "one serene and moonlight night, when all the waves rolled by like scrolls of silver; and, by their soft, suffusing seethings, made what seemed a silvery silence, not a solitude; on such a silent night a silvery jet was seen far in advance of the white bubbles at the bow. Lit up by the moon, it looked celestial; seemed some plumed and glittering god uprising from the sea." Fedallah first described this jet. (Chapter 51)

Although there was no whale there, the ghostly spout continued to appear almost every night.

> This solitary spout seemed forever luring us on. Nor with the immemorial superstition of their race, and in accordance with the pre-

[6] Dorothee Metlitsky Finkelstein, *Melville's Orienda* (New Haven: Yale University Press, 1961), pp. 223ff.

[7] Ibid., p. 232.

ternaturalness, as it seemed, which in many things invested the Pequod, were there wanting some of the seamen who swore that whenever and wherever descried; at however remote times, or in however far apart latitudes and longitudes, that unnearable spout was cast by one self-same whale; and that whale, Moby-Dick. For a time, there reigned, too, a sense of peculiar dread at this flitting apparition, as if it were treacherously beckoning us on and on, in order that the monster might turn round upon us, and rend us at last in the remotest and most savage seas. (Chapter 51)

The spirit spout is clearly related to Fedallah. It is seen shortly after he makes his appearance, and he is the first to observe it. The superstition, i.e., the unconscious, of the sailors connect the spout with Moby-Dick. Thus it is hinted that Fedallah, spirit spout, and Moby-Dick are interrelated as a kind of infernal trinity. The spirit spout is the guiding phantom or psychopomp leading the way to the encounter with the numinosum. The theme of a mysterious guiding factor leading the way into the unconscious is not uncommon in dreams and fairy tales. Fedallah and the spirit spout connected with him serve this purpose in *Moby-Dick*.

In Chapter 54, entitled "The Town-Ho's Story," we meet an apparent digression. However, on closer inspection, the Town-Ho's story is seen to be an integral part of the larger story; it presents another facet of the symbolic meaning of the white whale. The Town-Ho's story concerns a violent conflict that took place on the ship Town-Ho between Radney, the first mate, and Steelkilt, one of the seamen. Steelkilt is described as a man of great natural dignity and power. He "was a tall and noble animal with a head like a Roman," and with "a brain, and a heart, and a soul in him . . . which had made Steelkilt Charlemagne, had he been born son to Charlemagne's father." Radney, the first mate, was a petty, vicious man who could not endure Steelkilt's natural superiority. Radney was an example of the common occurrence "that when a person placed in command over his fellow-men finds one of them to be very significantly his superior in general pride of manhood, straightway against that man he conceives an unconquerable dislike and bitterness; and if he have a chance he will pull down and pulverize that subaltern's tower, and make a little heap of dust of it." (Chapter 54)

The gist of the story is that Radney deliberately insults Steelkilt and makes every effort to degrade him and destroy his personal dignity. As a consequence, Steelkilt nurtures a reaction of murderous vengeance and quietly makes plans to kill Radney. But just as Steelkilt's plans are ready to be carried out, the white whale Moby-Dick is sighted, and in the ensuing chase Radney is killed by the whale. Steelkilt's intended victim becomes instead the victim of Moby-Dick; "by a mysterious fatality, Heaven itself seemed to step in to take out of Steelkilt's hands into its own the damning thing he would have done." (Chapter 54)

It is evident that Melville means to equate Steelkilt's vengeful reaction with the white whale who carries out the actual avenging deed. When an individual's essential human dignity is attacked, as happened to Steelkilt, the deity within, the Self, is affronted; and contrary to all reasonable and personal considerations, it insists on executing nemesis. The white whale, the avenging deity of the collective psyche, manifests itself in Steelkilt's vengeance and punishes Radney for his violation of human dignity, which is likewise a violation of God.

A similar reaction is described in Melville's novel *White Jacket*. The narrator, White Jacket, had been accused of a wrong he did not commit, and the captain was threatening to have him flogged. Against this indignity White Jacket's inmost being rebelled, and he thought of making a mad dash against the captain that would send them both to their death in the sea.

> I but swung to an instinct in me—the instinct diffused through all animated nature, the same that prompts even a worm to turn under the heel. Locking souls with him, I meant to drag Captain Claret from this earthly tribunal of his to that of Jehovah, and let Him decide between us. . . . Nature has not implanted any power in man that was not meant to be exercised at times; . . . The privilege, inborn and unalienable, that every man has, of dying himself, and inflicting death upon another, was not given us without a purpose. These are the last resources of an insulted and unendurable existence. (*White Jacket*, Chapter 67)

In this passage, Melville speaks of the "instinct diffused through all animated nature" which seeks to preserve the integrity of the individual organism. The psychological equivalent of this instinct, that which preserves and promotes the integrity of our psychic being, is the urge to individuation. It derives from the Self and is experienced as a transpersonal power which transcends the ego. Indeed, all that is called instinct in biological terminology, when experienced psychologically, is best described as deity. The man who sacrifices his own life rather than submit to an intolerable indignity is operating out of a suprapersonal dynamism. Symbolically, he is acting out the "will of God," who will not have the central value of personality denied. From the standpoint of the persecuting oppressor whom he kills, the affronted man is acting as the avenging deity, the externalization of the oppressor's own unconscious which brings nemesis in reaction to hybris.

In the story of the conflict between Radney and Steelkilt, we have a capsule version, presented in the context of an interpersonal relationship, of the larger conflict between Ahab and Moby-Dick. Radney is even described in terms reminiscent of Ahab. Concerning Radney's compulsion to humiliate Steelkilt, it is said that "Radney was doomed and made mad." In his compulsion, Radney is called "the predestined mate" and "the infatuated man who sought to run more than halfway to meet his doom." All of these remarks could apply well to Ahab.

13 *LINKED ANALOGIES*

A LARGE middle section of *Moby-Dick* is devoted to detailed factual descriptions of the various aspects of whaling. This section is interesting from the factual standpoint alone, but Melville's intention exceeds mere fact. Scattered comments make it clear that the practical aspects of the whaling industry, and by extension all practical pursuits of man, have another level of meaning. Whaling, agriculture, manufacturing, building, etc., as practical business enterprises are but shadows in Plato's cave. Archetypal life meanings stand behind these commonplace pursuits. The key to this view is found in Ahab's remark, "O Nature, and O soul of man! how far beyond all utterances are your linked analogies! not the smallest atom stirs or lives on matter, but has its cunning duplicate in mind." (Chapter 70)

This is what is called the theory of correspondences. Emerson expresses the same idea. "Every natural fact is a symbol of some spiritual fact. Every appearance in nature corresponds to some state of mind, and that state of mind can only be described by presenting that natural appearance as its picture."[1]

The awareness of the "linked analogies" between the outer and inner worlds is evidence of conscious contact with the objective psyche, a contact which Melville repeatedly demonstrates. His factual chapters on whaling should therefore be read in this light. Take, for instance, the chapter on ambergris, a morbid secretion found in the bowels of sick whales. Melville remarks: "Now that the incorruption of this most fragrant ambergris should be found in the heart of such decay; is this nothing? Bethink thee of that saying of St. Paul in Corinthians, about corruption and incorruption; how that we are sown in dishonor but raised in glory." (Chapter 92) The book is filled with such linked analogies of the soul, some explicit, some implied. They make for a book of immense psychological richness that repays careful study. In Chapter 87, entitled "The Grand Armada," an impressive image is presented. A gigantic herd of thousands of whales has been encountered. Ishmael in his whale-boat finds himself caught up in this maelstrom of leviathans, and eventually the boat reaches the calm center of the concentric circular horde.

> We were now in that enchanted calm which they say lurks at the heart of every commotion. And still in the distracted distance we beheld the tumults of the outer concentric circles, and saw successive pods of whales, eight or ten in each, swiftly going round and round, like multiplied spans of horses in a ring. . . . But far beneath this wondrous world upon the surface, another and still stranger world met our eyes as we gazed over the side. For, suspended in those watery vaults, floated the forms of the nursing mothers of the whales, and those that by their enormous girth seemed shortly to become mothers. The lake, as I have hinted, was to a considerable depth exceedingly transparent; and as human infants while suckling will calmly and fixedly gaze away from the breast, as if leading two different lives at the time; and while yet drawing mortal nourishment, be still spiritually feasting, upon some unearthly reminiscence;—even so did the young of these whales seem looking up towards us, but not at us, as if we were but a bit of Gulf-weed in their newborn sight. . . . Some of the subtlest secrets of the

[1] "Nature," *The Writings of Ralph Waldo Emerson* (New York: Modern Library, 1940), p. 15.

seas seemed divulged to us in this enchanted pond. We saw young Leviathan amours in the deep.

And thus, though surrounded by circle upon circle of consternations and affrights, did these inscrutable creatures at the centre freely and fearlessly indulge in all peaceful concernments; yes, serenely revelled in dalliance and delight. But even so amid the tornadoed Atlantic of my being, do I myself still for ever centrally disport in mute calm; and while ponderous planets of unwaning woe revolve round me, deep down and deep inland there I still bathe me in eternal mildness of joy. (Chapter 87)

In this brilliantly expressed image of the calm, creative center of the tumultuous circle, we have the symbol of the spiral concentric whirlpool which appears at the end of the book as seen from inside. The circular horde of whales moving in concentric rings is a gigantic, living mandala, the center of which is the creative point of generation. A similar image appeared in the dream of a man undergoing analysis. The dreamer dreamt that he was at the home of the great male eels somewhere in the south Atlantic, the point to which eels from all over the world, following some mysterious instinct, come to breed. From the center of this great life mass, he watched billions of eels radiating in all directions as far as the horizon.[2]

Here again, we have a living mandala made up of the multitude of eels radiating from a central generative point. For the dreamer, this dream had a decisive healing effect. In general, the experience of the central spot of creation which this dream represents does have healing consequences.

The image of the living whale mandala which Ishmael penetrated to its center must be taken in conjunction with the spiral and whirlpool images of the final chapters. They are in fact two sides of the same psychic phenomenon, namely an encounter with the Self. The former image expresses the positive, healing effects of contact with the Self, the center of one's being. Although this aspect is not emphasized in *Moby-Dick*, it is definitely present. The last image of healing we encountered occurred when Ishmael's alienation was healed by Queequeg and Ishmael could say, "No more my splintered heart and maddened hand were turned against the wolfish world. This soothing savage had redeemed it." (Chapter 10) Since

[2] Reported by C. A. Meier in a private seminar in New York City. *Bulletin of the Analytical Psychology Club of New York*, January 1955.

then, Ahab has entered the picture, and Ishmael has become infected by his inflated and alienated state. But now, through contact with the creative center of the whale mandala, he is healed for a second time. The second circle of the spiral is completed. The appearance of this healing symbol is another evidence that the drama of *Moby-Dick* will not be an unmitigated tragedy. We shall encounter more evidence for this point later.

Ishmael's state of grace, in contact with the calm center, did not last long. The Pequod's mission would not permit it. A few chapters later, one night while Ishmael was standing at the helm, while the fiery try-works were melting down the whale, he had an ominous unconscious happening:

As to and fro, in their front, the harpooners wildly gesticulated with their huge pronged forks and dippers; as the wind howled on, and the sea leaped, and the ship groaned and dived, and yet steadfastly shot her red hell further and further into the blackness of the sea and the night, and scornfully champed the white bone in her mouth, and viciously spat round her on all sides; then the rushing Pequod, freighted with savages, and laden with fire, and burning a corpse, and plunging into that blackness of darkness, seemed the material counterpart of her monomaniac commander's soul.

But that night, in particular, a strange (and ever since inexplicable) thing occurred to me. Starting from a brief standing sleep, I was horribly conscious of something fatally wrong. The jaw-bone tiller smote my side, which leaned against it; in my ears was the low hum of sails, just beginning to shake in the wind; I thought my eyes were open; I was half-conscious of putting my fingers to the lids and mechanically stretching them still further apart. But, in spite of all this, I could see no compass before me to steer by; though it seemed but a minute since I had been watching the card, by the steady binnacle lamp illuminating it. Nothing seemed before me but a jet of gloom, now and then made ghastly by flashes of redness. Uppermost was the impression, that whatever swift, rushing thing I stood on was not so much bound to any haven ahead as rushing from all havens astern. A stark, bewildered feeling, as of death, came over me. Convulsively my hands grasped the tiller, but with the crazy conceit that the tiller was, somehow, in some enchanted way, inverted. My God! what is the matter with me? thought I. Lo! in my brief sleep I had turned myself about, and was fronting the ship's stern, with my back to her prow and the compass. In an instant I faced back, just in time to prevent the vessel from flying up into the wind, and very probably capsizing her. How glad and how grateful the relief from this unnatural hallucination of the night, and the fatal contingency of being brought by the lee! (Chapter 96)

This "unnatural hallucination of the night" carries a meaning. Ishmael's unconscious is attempting to turn away from the attitude that is plunging him into "the blackness of darkness." When one fails to permit an inner reaction to become conscious, it may then seize our bodily functions and force an expression through them, concretizing the image it wishes to convey. So it is with psychosomatic illnesses, and so it is with the majority of so-called accidents. We know that certain people are accident-prone, which means that their unconscious has a tendency to express itself by making accidents. Unless or until the psychological meaning of such apparent accidents becomes conscious, they will continue perhaps to a fatal outcome. We learned early that Ishmael is the type who attempts to deal with all distressing facts by forgetting about them. We noted his previous remark, "when a man suspects any wrong, it sometimes happens that if he be already involved in the matter, he insensibly strives to cover up his suspicions even from himself." It is this repressive attitude that is apt to evoke "accidents." If we are wise, we will reflect on each apparent accident that befalls us. It will carry an unconscious message just as does a dream. Ishmael came perilously close to having the unconscious cause an accident. As we are all apt to do when we awake from a nightmare, he exclaims in relief that it is "only a dream" and draws this superficial conclusion: "Tomorrow, in the natural sun, the skies will be bright; those who glared like devils in the forking flames, the morn will show in far other, at least gentler, relief; the glorious golden, glad sun, the only true lamp— all others but liars!" (Chapter 96)

The messages of the night are too distressing, and so they go unheeded. In spite of this superficial reaction, Ishmael does draw some significant conclusions from the hallucination, although they are almost lost in the ambiguity of his total response. "Look not too long in the face of the fire, O man! . . . Give not thyself up . . . to the fire, lest it invert thee, deaden thee; as for the time it did me. There is a wisdom that is woe; but there is a woe that is madness." (Chapter 96)

These are remarks that Melville himself might well take to heart. A short time previously, Ishmael had experienced the positive effects of the whale mandala's center. These could have helped balance the Pequod's heavy freight of woe, but instead they seem to have been lost. Again Ishmael, with Ahab, is gazing transfixed at the negative side of life which can lead to the "woe that is madness." The unconscious reaction that turns him around in the opposite direction is attempting to compensate for the unbalanced picture of life into which Ishmael had fallen.

At the beginning of the voyage, it will be recalled, when Ahab had the crew swear to join him in the hunt for Moby-Dick, he nailed a gold doubloon to the mainmast and promised it to the first man to spy the white whale. The circular golden doubloon is a mandala and hence an image of the Self. It is stated that the doubloon is "the white whale's talisman," thereby establishing an organic connection between the symbolic meaning of the coin and that of the whale. This provides added evidence for the conclusion previously reached that the white whale is a symbol of the Self. Now, in Chapter 94, each person confronts the doubloon and expresses what it means to him. Each projects his own psychic contents on it and thereby reveals his own attitude and relation toward the Self. On the coin is seen: "the likeness of three Andes' summits; from one a flame; a tower on another; on the third a crowing cock; while arching over all was a segment of the partitioned zodiac; the signs of all marked with their usual cabalistics, and the keystone sun entering the equinoctial point at Libra." (Chapter 99)

The zodiac is itself a mandala Self-image projected on the heaven and divided into the twelve archetypal zones or houses. Within this zodiacal circle on the coin there are three mountains. Mountains have always represented the abode of the sky or spirit gods and the place where man and god meet. The cosmic mountain occupies the center of the world and hence is called the world navel. The number three suggests the masculine trinity, and other images re-enforce the masculine emphasis. Fire, tower, cock, and sun are all alternative expressions of the masculine spirit principle.

First to approach the coin is Ahab who says:

> There's something ever egotistical in mountain-tops and towers, and all
> other grand and lofty things; look here,—three peaks as proud as
> Lucifer. The firm tower, that is Ahab; the volcano, that is Ahab; the
> courageous, the undaunted, and victorious fowl, that, too, is Ahab; all

are Ahab; and this round gold is but the image of the rounder globe, which, like a magician's glass, to each and every man in turn but mirrors back his own mysterious self. Great pains, small gains for those who ask the world to solve them; it cannot solve itself. Methinks now this coined sun wears a ruddy face; but see! aye, he enters the sign of storms, the equinox! and but six months before he wheeled out of a former equinox at Aries! From storm to storm! So be it, then. Born in throes, 'tis fit that man should live in pains and die in pangs! So be it, then! Here's stout stuff for woe to work on. So be it, then. (Chapter 99)

If we did not already know it, Ahab's inflation would now stand revealed. He identifies himself with the three proud mountain peaks, the ego is identified with the Self. Such a psychic condition is indeed a stormy one, and so Ahab sees the storms to come. Here Ahab has a mirror for Medusa, but he is too blind to use it.

Next Starbuck inspects the coin and observes:

A dark valley between three mighty, heaven-abiding peaks, that almost seem the Trinity, in some faint earthly symbol. So in this vale of Death, God girds us round; and over all our gloom, the sun of Righteousness still shines a beacon and a hope. If we bend down our eyes, the dark vale shows her mouldy soil; but if we lift them, the bright sun meets our glance half way, to cheer. Yet, oh, the great sun is no fixture; and if, at midnight, we would fain snatch some sweet solace from him, we gaze for him in vain! This coin speaks wisely, mildly, truly, but still sadly to me. I will quit it, lest Truth shake me falsely. (Chapter 99)

Where Ahab sees the mountain peaks, Starbuck sees the dark valley, the moldy soil of the vale of death. This valor-ruined man whose soul is overmanned is caught in the valley of Ahab's mountains. He dare not stay to read the full meaning of the coin for fear of being shaken by it.

Stubb notices only the zodiacal signs and lacking any imagination of his own must go to an almanac to read their meanings. Thus it is with the sensation function which can establish no more than their factual associations. Flask, the least developed of all, sees nothing in the sixteen-dollar gold coin but nine hundred and sixty cigars at two cents a cigar. Even his arithmetic is wrong. All Flask knows is that he likes cigars. Queequeg views the coin and compares it with his own tattoo markings. As already noted, Queequeg carries something of the original wholeness of the primordial Self, hence he sees a naïve oneness between his own body markings and the doubloon mandala. Fedallah pays obeisance to the doubloon by bowing down to it. This indicates that despite his diabolical aspects, he is related to wholeness. In his role as "avenging angel," he is in the service of the Self.

Finally, Pip, the demented colored boy, comes to view the coin. This was the boy who had jumped in fear from a whaleboat for a second time and had been left in the sea too long before being picked up. But Melville says it better:

> The sea had jeeringly kept his finite body up, but drowned the infinite of his soul. Not drowned entirely, though. Rather carried down alive to wondrous depths, where strange shapes of the unwarped primal world glided to and fro before his passive eyes; and the miser-merman, Wisdom, revealed his hoarded heaps; and among the joyous, heartless, ever-juvenile eternities, Pip saw the multitudinous, God-omnipresent, coral insects, that out of the firmament of waters heaved the colossal orbs. He saw God's foot upon the treadle of the loom, and spoke it; and therefore his shipmates called him mad. So man's insanity is heaven's sense, and wandering from all mortal reason, man comes at last to that celestial thought, which, to reason, is absurd and frantic. (Chapter 93)

Pip is an example of a well-known archetypal figure, the fool. One thinks, for instance, of *Parsifal* and the fool in *King Lear*. The figure of the fool represents that orientation which although apparently stupid and inept in relation to the conscious world of material expediency, is in tune with the eternal verities of the objective psyche. It is the meaning of Paul when he said:

> "If there is anyone among you who fancies himself wise—wise, I mean, by the standard of this passing age—he must become a fool to gain true wisdom. For the wisdom of this world is folly in God's sight." (1 Cor. 3:18–19)

This is the meaning of Pip's foolishness and insanity. The ambiguity between wisdom and foolishness had just been voiced by Stubb in response to Flask's reaction to the coin. "Shall I call that wise or foolish, now; if it be really wise it has a foolish look to it; yet if it be really foolish, then has it a sort of wiseish look to it." (Chapter 99) But now comes Pip, the demented fool of the ship, and provides the wisest answer to the meaning of the doubloon: "Here's the ship's navel, this doubloon here, and they are all on fire to unscrew it. But, unscrew your navel, and what's the consequence?" (Chapter 99)

The image of the world-navel is a widespread one. It is a parallel to the central generative point within the whale mandala previously discussed. The world-navel corresponds to the central point or axis where man and god, personal and suprapersonal meet. In Greece, Delphi, the site of the oracle, was considered the navel of the world. Zeus released two eagles flying in opposite directions. They met at Delphi, establishing it as the world-navel—the place where opposites meet. In Indian myth, Mount Meru was the center of the world.[3] The world-navel represents the central source of life energy deriving from the gods, i.e., the transpersonal psyche. To unscrew the navel would hence cut one off from that life source and would be self-destructive. Thus, the Pequod continues its suicidal course.

Sometime later, it was discovered that oil from the barrels stored in the hold was leaking. Ahab refuses to spend time searching for the leak and gives a vivid description of his own psychic state: "Let it leak! I'm all aleak myself. Aye! leaks in leaks! not only full of leaky casks, but those leaky casks are in a leaky ship; and that's a far worse plight than the Pequod's man. Yet I don't stop to plug my leak; for who can find it in the deep-loaded hull; or how hope to plug it, even if found, in this life's howling gale?" (Chapter 109)

Ahab is indeed "all aleak." The unconscious is leaking into his ego. However, this remark is the first indication that a modicum of self-awareness is beginning to dawn on Ahab. Starbuck, who brought him the information about the leaking oil, is ordered angrily back on deck. As he leaves, Starbuck replies, "Let Ahab beware of Ahab; beware of thyself, old man." Again, some measure of the self-reflective capacity breaks in, for Ahab muses, "What's that he said—Ahab beware of Ahab—there's something there." And in fact, Ahab reverses himself and orders a search for the leak. This is the first of several incidents indicating a growing self-awareness in Ahab which begins to humanize him even if it is not sufficient to avert his tragic end.

[3] For an extensive discussion of the "symbolism of the center," see Mircea Eliade, *Images and Symbols* (New York: Sheed and Ward, 1961), pp. 27ff.

14 THE PACT WITH THE DEVIL

As THE PEQUOD approached the cruising grounds where it is expected that Moby-Dick will be found, Ahab has the blacksmith make him a special harpoon of the hardest steel to use against the white whale. For the final tempering, he asks the three harpooners for some of their blood, and into this he plunges the heated barbs. "*'Ego non baptizo te in nomine patris, sed in nomine diaboli!'* deliriously howled Ahab, as the malignant iron scorchingly devoured the baptismal blood." (Chapter 113)

This ritual confirms what has been suspected all along, that Ahab's pact with Fedallah is a pact with the devil. First of all, we note that Ahab does not use the full formula of Christian baptism. The complete ritual statement is, "I baptize you in the name of the Father and of the Son and of the Holy Spirit." Ahab omits reference to the Son and the Holy Spirit. This suggests that his psychological state corresponds symbolically to the pre-Christian period. Ahab's image of deity is the Old Testament Yahweh.

The Christian trinity of Father, Son, and Holy Spirit is one of many threefold images symbolizing the developmental stages of psychic growth.[1] The first three numbers have important psychological symbolism. Number one as the first and original number is not, strictly speaking, a number at all. "One" as unity and totality exists prior to the awareness of numbers, which requires a capacity to distinguish between separate, discrete entities. Thus "one" corresponds symbolically to the original state of wholeness prior to creation and the separation of things. "Two" is the first real number, since with it is born the possibility of discriminating one thing from another. "Two" symbolizes the act of creation, the emergence of the ego from the original state of unity. "Two" causes opposition. It represents a state of conflict. "Three," however, is the sum of one and two and unites them both within itself. It is the reconciling symbol that resolves the conflict state of two.[2]

[1] Edinger, *op. cit.,* pp. 179ff.
[2] C. G. Jung, *Psychology and Religion: West and East*, CW 11 (Princeton, N.J.: Princeton University Press, 1970), par. 180.

The three terms in the Christian trinity, considered as phases of psychic development, can be equated with the symbolical meanings of numbers one, two, and three just presented. The Age of the Father (one) is the state of original oneness with life, without "doubt" or doubleness of mind. The Age of the Son (two) is a state of inner conflict in which the ego is separated from its original ground of being. It is a state of alienation which longs for redemption or salvation. The Age of the Holy Spirit (three) is the stage of reconciliation. The opposites "Father" and "Son" have been connected by a third, the Holy Spirit, which provides reciprocal communication and a release from the irreconcilable conflict of opposites in stage two.[3]

Ahab omits the trinitarian formula of baptism because it does not correspond to his psychological state. He is in stage two, the state of conflict and alienation. He experiences himself as the son of the father who can maintain his identity only by defiance, by insisting that two exist, not just one. Like Job, Ahab is rebelling against the "age of the father."

The phrase, "I baptize you not in the name of the father but in the name of the devil," takes on special significance because it appears in a letter Melville wrote to Hawthorne shortly after finishing *Moby-Dick:* "Shall I send you a fin of the 'whale' by way of a specimen mouthful? The tail is not yet cooked, though the hell-fire in which the whale book is boiled might not unreasonably have cooked it ere this. This is the book's motto (the secret one), Ego non baptiso te in nomine—but make out the rest yourself."[4]

Not long afterward, in another letter to Hawthorne, Melville writes, "I have written a wicked book, and feel spotless as the lamb."[5]

It is clear enough that Ahab has made a pact with the devil in his vengeful quest for the white whale, but these passages from Melville's letters indicate that Melville himself felt he had made a pact with the devil in writing *Moby-Dick.* How else can we explain the clear statement that the book has been baptized in the name of the Devil? We know that the theme of "a pact with the devil" was on Melville's mind, because he wrote notes outlining a story concerning a compact with the devil in 1849 on a blank page of his new edition

[3] Ibid., pars. 201ff.
[4] Metcalf, *op. cit.,* p. 111.
[5] Ibid., p. 129.

of Shakespeare.[6] What some believe to be rough notes for *Moby-Dick* are in that same edition of Shakespeare:

> *Ego non baptizo te in nomine Patris et Filii et*
> *Spiritus Sancti—sed in nomine Diaboli—*madness is
> indefinable—
> It and right reason extremes of one,
> —not the (black art) Goetic but Theurgic magic—
> seeks converse with the Intelligence, Power, the Angel.[7]

This is a mysterious and enigmatic passage. According to Webster, the word *goetic* means pertaining to necromancy or the black art. *Theurgy* means literally a divine work. It was a term used by certain Neoplatonists referring to a kind of occult art "in which knowledge of divine marks, or signatures, in nature, is held to be capable of evoking or utilizing the aid of divine and beneficent spirits." We can conclude therefore, as does Olson,[8] that the distinction Melville makes between Goetic and Theurgic magic corresponds approximately to the ancient conventional distinction between black magic and white magic. He is thus affirming white magic and denying black magic as a method of "seeking converse" with the suprapersonal psychic powers. However, if this is Melville's meaning, why does he in the first sentence speak of baptizing in the name of the devil? That could only be black magic. In fact, there is no easy distinction between black and white magic. We are reminded of the definition of the devil in *Faust*—that power that "always wills the bad, and always works the good." (Scene iii)

Before going into this paradoxical point, let us consider the psychological meaning of magic. Magic, whether used for good or ill, is the effort to evoke and utilize for personal ends the secret, divine, or supernatural agencies of life. Understood psychologically, it is the effort to activate and use the transpersonal energies of the objective psyche. Although magic is a superstitious fallacy when it is used to control the outer world, it is a demonstrable reality when understood as referring to the inner world of the unconscious psyche. By the process of imagination, it can put one in contact with the archetypal energies of life. To put it simply, the psychic equivalent of magic is imagination.

[6] Leyda, *op. cit.*, p. 297.
[7] Olson, *op. cit.*, p. 52.
[8] Ibid., p. 56.

Traditionally, magic has been termed "black" if it is used to promote destructive ends motivated by hate or vengeance, and "white" if it is used for benevolent, life-promoting ends. However, this distinction between black and white magic is an ambiguous one. A dream reported by Jung is relevant here. It is that of a theology student who was having doubts about his faith: The dreamer

> was standing in the presence of a handsome old man dressed entirely in *black*. He knew it was the *white* magician. This personage had just addressed him at considerable length, but the dreamer could no longer remember what it was about. He had only retained the closing words: "And for this we need the help of the *black* magician." At that moment the door opened and in came another old man exactly like the first, except that he was dressed in *white*. He said to the white magician [who was dressed in black], "I need your advice". . . . The black magician [who was dressed in white] then began to relate his story.

His adventures concluded with his discovery of the lost keys of *paradise*. But now the black magician (dressed in white) needed the help of the white magician (dressed in black) because the former did not know what to do with keys of paradise.[9]

This dream makes several points that are pertinent to our subject. First of all, the black and white magicians are in disguise. The white magician is dressed in black, and the black magician is dressed in white. Thus, one cannot tell by superficial appearance which is which. Indeed, if he goes by appearances he will be deceived. Hence, what appears to be black magic may really be white magic, and the converse is also true. To use psychological terms, this means that in the working of the imagination what appears to be hate may actually be love, and what appears to be love may be hate. Beyond this, the dream says that the black and white magicians have a reciprocal need for one another. The black magician has the keys of paradise but doesn't know what to do with them, while the white magician knows how to use the keys but doesn't have them. Black and white, good and evil are thus reciprocal entities each of which needs the other. Do we not have a parallel here with the ambiguous color symbolism of the white whale?

The white magician needs the black magician. Love needs hate. In fact, the latter has the lost keys to paradise, i.e., is closest to the

[9] Jung, *The Archetypes and the Collective Unconscious*, par. 71.

original wholeness and source of creative energies. Here is a problem that Melville was to grapple with all his life. Consciously, Melville could not accept his own intense negative reactions, his hate. Hear this passage from *Mardi* (Chapter 13) which follows a description of the disagreeable nature of sharks. "As well hate a seraph, as a shark. Both were made by the same hand. . . . We know not what we do when we hate. . . . hate is a thankless thing. So, let us only hate hatred; . . . Ah! the easiest way is the best; and to hate, a man must work hard. Love is a delight; but hate a torment. And haters are thumbscrews, Scotch boots, and Spanish inquisitors to themselves. In five words . . . he who hates is a fool."

But hate cannot be disposed of so easily. Melville puts it more accurately in a later poem:

> Nothing may help or heal
> While Amor incensed remembers wrong.
> Vindictive, not himself he'll spare;
> For scope to give his vengeance play
> Himself he'll blaspheme and betray.[10]

Hatred is the anguish of a wounded god—Amor. This is a much truer and deeper view of the nature of hate. Hatred is not to be banished to repression by calling it foolish; rather to face it leads one to the encounter with the god of love himself. Here then is another facet to the symbolic meaning of Ahab—he is the wounded god of love, Eros. If the capacity to love has been damaged, restoration is possible only by living through the experience of the symptom of that damage, hatred. I am reminded of the Indian aphoristic question, "Who takes longer to reach perfection, the man who loves God, or the man who hates him?" And the answer is: "He who loves God takes seven reincarnations to reach perfection; and he who hates God takes only three, for he who hates God will think of him more than he who loves him."[11]

Love and hate are a pair of opposites. If one side of a pair of opposites is ruled out, the dynamism of development, which requires a tension between opposite poles, is arrested. Psychic energy is dammed up and poisons the personality with increasing bitterness. In such a case, the opportunity to feel and express hatred may have

[10] "After the Pleasure Party," *Collected Poems*, p. 221.
[11] Jung, *The Archetypes of the Collective Unconscious*, par. 76.

a releasing effect on the emotional life. This is commonly observed in psychotherapy. If value and meaning can be attached to the feeling of hatred—as by considering it the distress of a wounded god —the individual may then be released to experience love as well. Hatred has dangerous and destructive consequences only when its source is repressed. It takes on a rigid, compulsive quality only when the conscious personality has an idealistic prejudice against the negative pole of the feeling life, that is when the psyche is split into irreconcilable halves.

In one book, Melville allowed himself to write out of his repressed hatred, and this book is his masterpiece. With this book, he experienced a power and depth of imagination completely unmatched in any of his other works and discovered for himself that it is the black magician that has the keys to paradise. Melville called *Moby-Dick* a wicked book, baptized in the name of the devil, because it was the product of his own pact with the devil. The devil is a personification of all those aspects of an individual's psychology which contradict his conscious, ideal image of himself and which therefore must be repressed. For a conventional Christian consciousness, the devil will be all that is unChristlike—sexuality, power, self-interest, and material desires as opposed to spiritual ones. All of these were part of Melville's repressed psychology as well as part of the repressed collective psychology of his time. Over and beyond childhood trauma, Ahab's violent hatred derived from a brutal mistreatment of natural life energies by a conscious ideal. In this sense, Murray is right when he suggests that one of the meanings of the white whale is the cultural superego, that body of collective ideals of behavior derived largely from Puritan Christianity.[12] Melville was thus living out and embodying in living images a collective as well as a personal problem.

At a certain phase of psychic development, one is obliged to accept and grant value to those repressed aspects of his own psychology which previously he considered to be the realm of the devil. Thereby he enters a pact with the devil. Failure to do so can mean an arrest of growth and loss of contact with the energies of life—the sterile state that Faust was in before he invoked Mephistopheles. However, the dangers of such a course are evident in the image itself. The devil is still the devil, and he is a psychic reality. Such a

[12] Murray, "In Nomine Diaboli," *Moby Dick Centennial Essays*, p. 15.

course is a heterodox, individual way that can receive no collective sanction. As in the encounter with the alchemical Mercurius, who has symbolic affinities with Lucifer, one may be either poisoned or healed. If there is a latent tendency to dissociation, letting down the bars of repression can provoke an actual psychosis. Melville came perilously close to this in the aftermath of writing *Moby-Dick*.

Melville's pact with the devil was his decision to give artistic expression to his hatred, to embody it in a noble, tragic figure—"a mighty pageant creature." There is evidence that Melville had been reading Milton's *Paradise Lost* not long before writing *Moby-Dick* and various commentators have noted the similarities between Ahab and Milton's Satan. According to the Christian myth, Satan was expelled from heaven, and this led to the splitting of the universe into two irreconcilable opposites. This is a picture of the split in the Christian's individual and collective psyche. This separation of opposites was a necessary step in the evolution of the god-image. It was certainly an advance from the Yahweh we see in the Book of Job and other parts of the Old Testament.

But the differentiating dissociation between God and Satan has long since served its purpose. The psyche of modern man is suffering from the effects of that split and is in need rather of a conscious reconciliation between these opposing archetypal principles. This is the message of the dream of the black and white magicians. Since Satan represents all aspects of life which have been rejected and depreciated, and since the need of the modern mind is to reclaim and redeem that part of itself which has been alienated from consciousness by the Christian dissociation, we therefore find many of the most creative figures of the nineteenth century engaged in the process of reclaiming for consciousness the very aspects of life which has been cast out with the devil in the Christian myth. Goethe created his modern myth of Faust involving the reclaiming of unregenerate desirousness. Marx reasserted the reality of the economic, that is the material as opposed to the spiritual motivations of man. Darwin re-established the primacy of the biological survival mechanisms. Nietzsche rehabilitated and glorified the will to power. Freud reclaimed the energies of repressed sexuality. Each of these pioneers spent his life exploring the devil's territory, according to Christian topography, in an effort to reclaim and redeem for conscious use the repressed human energies which had been consigned to hell by the Christian dissociation. Perhaps the most important of all the functions to be reclaimed from hell is that of the creative imagination. Since the imagination is a function of the total personality, it must include the repressed primitive aspect consigned to the devil by Christian consciousness. (Both Queequeg and Fedallah are carriers of wholeness.) Imagination and creativity are apt to seem Satanic, since in their very nature they transcend the separation of the opposites. From the standpoint of a limited attitude, that which is beyond good and evil will seem to be evil. Hence Blake could write, "The reason Milton wrote in fetters when he wrote of Angels & Gods, and at liberty when of Devils & Hell, is because he was a true Poet and of the Devil's party without knowing it."[13]

All these considerations apply to Melville and serve to elucidate the meaning of his pact with the devil. Probably his major concern was to release the energies of the creative imagination. As James Kirsch observes, the writing of *Moby-Dick* was an experiment in active imagination. This is the psychological theurgy that "seeks converse with the Intelligence, Power, the Angel"[14]—namely, the collective unconscious. That Melville discovered and used the process of active imagination essentially as we know it, is proved by a passage in *Mardi*. Lombardo, mentioned in the quotation, is a fictional representation of Melville as writer. "All men are inspired; fools are inspired . . . [you are] inspired; for the essence of all ideas is infused. Of ourselves, we originate nothing. When Lombardo set about his work, he knew not what it would become. He did not build himself in with plans; he wrote right on; and so doing, got deeper and deeper into himself; and like a resolute traveler, plunging through baffling woods, at last was rewarded for his toils." (Chapter 180)

The two basic insights on which the process of active imagination is based are here presented with clarity. The first is that all ideas and images that come to us are "infused," that is, come from a source other than the ego. We do not make them up. The second point is that we can explore these "infused" images by letting them come

---

[13] "The Marriage of Heaven and Hell," *The Poetry and Prose of William Blake,* David V. Erdman, ed. (New York: Doubleday & Company, Inc., 1965), p. 35.
[14] James Kirsch, "The Enigma of Moby Dick," *Journal of Analytical Psychology,* III (1958), p. 132.

as did Lombardo, who "wrote right on." Jung, the first to describe active imagination as a specific technique, speaks of it as follows: It is

> a method of introspection for observing the stream of interior images. One concentrates one's attention on some impressive but unintelligible dream image, or on a spontaneous visual impression, and observes changes taking place in it. Meanwhile, of course, all criticism must be suspended and the happenings observed and noted with absolute objectivity. Obviously, too, the objection that the whole thing is "arbitrary" or "thought up" must be set aside, since it springs from the anxiety of an ego-consciousness which brooks no master besides itself in its own house. In other words, it is the inhibition exerted by the conscious mind on the unconscious.
>
> Under these conditions, long and often very dramatic series of fantasies ensue. The advantage of this method is that it brings a mass of unconscious material to light. Drawing, painting and modelling can be used to the same end. Once a visual series has become dramatic, it can easily pass over into the auditive or linguistic sphere and give rise to dialogues and the like. With slightly pathological individuals, and particularly in the not infrequent cases of latent schizophrenia, the method may in certain circumstances, prove to be rather dangerous and therefore requires medical control. It is based on a deliberate weakening of the conscious mind and its inhibiting effect, which either limits or suppresses the unconscious.[15]

This method allows to emerge whatever image is present. Inhibiting conscious judgment is set aside. No question is asked whether a given image derives from God or the devil, since such a question would be a device of the ego to accept only what suits its own preconceptions. One can easily understand why Melville, living in the United States in 1851 and using such a procedure on himself, might well feel that he was making a pact with the devil. Such a procedure had absolutely no collective sanction. It was necessarily a guilty secret to be discussed with no one. The idea must have constantly haunted Melville that in this way lies madness. But he took as his hypothesis that madness and right reason are extremes of one—that is, reconcilable opposites. I can only agree with Kirsch when he comments on "the extraordinary courage which Melville demon-

---

[15] Jung, *The Archetypes and the Collective Unconscious*, pars. 319–20.

strated by starting the journey on that ocean which we now call the unconscious. He was truly a modern man."[16]

We must note, however, the mistakes that Melville made in his use of active imagination. Courage and recklessness should not be confused. There was something wild and rash in the way Melville proceeded. Like Ahab, he was trying to storm the gates of heaven with an inflated urgency that was dangerous. He went too fast. He "wrote right on" and did not stop to assimilate consciously the personal meaning of the images that flooded in on him. Here his weak relation to the masculine Logos principle is evident. He became possessed by the stream of autonomous imagery and did not spend sufficient effort in establishing a conscious standpoint with which to assimilate it. In the words of Shakespeare, "When valour preys on reason, it eats the sword it fights with."[17]

> Now he'll outstare the lightning. To be furious
> Is to be frightened out of fear, and in that mood
> The dove will peck the estridge. I see still
> A diminution in our captain's brain
> Restores his heart. When valour preys on reason,
> It eats the sword it fights with. I will seek
> Some way to leave him.

15 ENCOUNTER WITH THE NUMINOSUM

FOLLOWING THE RITUAL of baptizing Ahab's harpoon, the pace of the drama quickens. The ship is approaching "the season on the line" where Moby-Dick is expected to be found. A rapid series of events presage the approaching climax. First, the Pequod meets the Bachelor, a happy ship that is loaded with sperm oil and headed home. The jolly captain when asked if he has seen the white whale replies, "No; only heard of him; but don't believe in him at all." The Bachelor represents one-dimensional worldly success, untroubled by the deeper mysteries of life, in fact not believing in their existence. Ahab had once said of himself, "I can ne'er enjoy. Gifted

---

[16] Kirsch, *op. cit.*, p. 133.

[17] *Antony and Cleopatra*, III, xiii. The whole speech of Enobarbus' protesting Antony's rashness is relevant to Ahab:

with the high perception, I lack the low, enjoying power." (Chapter 37) The Bachelor is the opposite orientation—gifted with the enjoying power, lacking the high perception. As pointed out by Merlin Bowen,[1] throughout his writings Melville seems to use the term bachelor to describe the naive optimism of the once-born man who has not encountered the dark side of life. In his story, "The Paradise of Bachelors," he describes this type. "The thing called pain, the bugbear styled trouble—those two legends seemed preposterous to their bachelor imaginations. . . . how could they suffer themselves to be imposed upon by such monkish fables? Pain! Trouble! . . . No such thing—Pass the sherry, sir."[2]

The bachelor to life is the immature and uncommitted one of whatever age. The one who acknowledges no life responsibilities other than the fulfillment of his own personal satisfactions. Such a one does not even believe in the existence of Moby-Dick. Ahab, on the contrary, granted no place for his personal satisfaction. And although he put up a defiant front, it was evident that he was nostalgically affected by the homeward bound Bachelor, because shortly later he was seen gazing at a small vial of Nantucket sand taken from his pocket—a small indication that his frozen feelings were beginning to thaw.

While spending the night in a whaleboat beside a dead whale (Chapter 117), Ahab had a recurrent dream of hearses. It worried him. He feared that it presaged his own death. Such a dream has two possible interpretations. It may signify the imminent death of some part of the personality, an old attitude. This would be a psychological death, a prelude to the birth of a new attitude. The death dream would then have a positive, transformative implication. However, there are also dreams which give a forewarning of actual death. Lincoln had such a dream shortly before his assassination. He told it to a gathering on April 11, 1865, three days before he was shot:

> About ten days ago, I retired very late. I had been waiting up for important dispatches. I could not have been long in bed when I fell into a slumber, for I was weary. I soon began to dream. There seemed to be a death-like stillness about me. Then I heard subdued sobs, as if a num-

[1] Merlin Bowen, *The Long Encounter* (Chicago: University of Chicago Press, 1960), pp. 67ff.
[2] *Selected Writings of Herman Melville* (New York: Modern Library, 1952), pp. 193ff.

ber of people were weeping. I thought I left my bed and wandered downstairs.

There the silence was broken by the same pitiful sobbing, but the mourners were invisible. I went from room to room. No living person was in sight, but the same mournful sounds of distress met me as I passed along. It was light in all the rooms; every object was familiar to me, but where were all the people who were grieving as if their hearts would break?

I was puzzled and alarmed. What could be the meaning of all this? Determined to find the cause of a state of things so mysterious and so shocking, I kept on until I arrived in the East Room, which I entered. There I met with a sickening surprise. Before me was a catafalque, on which rested a corpse in funeral vestments. Around it were stationed soldiers who were acting as guards; and there was a throng of people, some gazing mournfully upon the corpse, whose face was covered, others weeping pitifully.

"Who is dead in the White House?" I demanded of one of the soldiers.

"The President," was his answer. "He was killed by an assassin."

Then came a loud burst of grief from the crowd which awoke me from my dream. I slept no more that night, and, although it was only a dream, I have been strangely annoyed by it ever since.[3]

This dream of Lincoln's is a particularly striking example of premonitory dreams. They are not particularly rare and many more examples could be educed. Jung reports several in his memoirs. The existence of such phenomena indicates that at some level the unconscious psyche transcends the conscious categories of time and space. Such happenings are disturbing because they contradict our rational *Weltanschauung*. Many, therefore, prefer to shut their eyes to these facts by calling them meaningless coincidences. But the facts remain and bear witness to the uncanny depths of the psyche.

As events demonstrated, Ahab's dream was one of the premonitory variety. Ahab sensed this but allowed himself to be reassured by Fedallah's prophecy. Fedallah promised him that "ere thou couldst die on this voyage, two hearses must verily be seen by thee on the sea; the first not made by mortal hands; and the visible wood of the last one must be grown in America. . . . Though it come

[3] Jim Bishop, *The Day Lincoln Was Shot* (New York: Harper & Brothers, 1955), pp. 55–56.

to the last, I shall still go before thee thy pilot. . . . Take another pledge, old man. . . . Hemp only can kill thee." (Chapter 117)

Fedallah is here serving as the oracle that prophesies a predetermined fate. Certain conditions must be fulfilled before Ahab can die. We are reminded of Macbeth, for whom similar conditions were laid down by the three witches:

> . . . none of woman born
> Shall harm Macbeth.
>
> . . . .
>
> Macbeth shall never vanquished be until
> Great Birnam wood to high Dunsinane hill
> Shall come against him. (IV. i.)

Ahab and Macbeth make the same mistake. Both arrogantly assume the prophecy is telling them they are invulnerable. Macbeth replies, "That will never be; Who can impress the forest, bid the tree unfix his earth-bound root?" (IV. i.), Ahab reacts in a similar vein, to the prophecy that hemp only can kill him. "The gallows, ye mean—I am immortal then, on land and on sea" (Chapter 117). Frightened Ahab grasps pitifully at the wish-born illusion that he understands the prophecy. He fails to reflect on what it means that his fate is predetermined. It means that no conscious freedom or choice is operating. He is living out a mythological role the pattern of which is fixed. Only consciousness of this fact could alter it, and this Ahab lacks.

In the following chapter (118), the destructive pace increases. Ahab has a tantrum over the limitations of the quadrant.

"Foolish toy! babies' plaything of haughty admirals, and commodores, and captains; the world brags of thee, of thy cunning and might; but what after all canst thou do, but tell the poor, pitiful point, where thou thyself happenest to be on this wide planet, and the hand that holds thee; no! not one jot more! Thou canst not tell where one drop of water or one grain of sand will be to-morrow noon; and yet with thy impotence thou insultest the sun! Science! Curse thee, thou vain toy; and cursed be all the things that cast man's eyes aloft to that heaven, whose live vividness but scorches him, as these old eyes are even now scorched with thy light, O sun! Level by nature to this earth's horizon are the glances of man's eyes; not shot from the crown of his head, as if God had meant him to gaze on his firmament. Curse thee, thou quadrant!" dashing it to the deck, "no longer will I guide my earthly way by thee."

This is a startling outburst that requires some explanation. By using a quadrant to measure the elevation of the sun, the mariner can determine his latitude. Ahab's angry affect is directed against the limitations of the quadrant, which can only tell him where he is, not where he will be. He is even more incensed against its presumed vanity and haughtiness—"with thy impotence thou insultest the sun." Who was it that said "I'd strike the sun if it insulted me"? Ahab himself. Whenever we observe an excessive affect reaction to a person or an object, we can suspect a psychological projection to be operating. Such is the case here. Ahab is berating the quadrant for its pride and presumption. But the pride and presumption are Ahab's.

Ahab lectures the quadrant, telling it that man's view is meant to be a horizontal one. If God had expected man to gaze incessantly at the sky he would have put his eyes in the top of his head. As with all gratuitous lectures and advice, the content is most applicable to the speaker. These are the facts that Ahab needs to recognize in himself. Although the destruction of the quadrant is a foolish act due to a misplacement of anger, the fact that Ahab is experiencing a powerful reaction against pride and presumption is highly significant. It means that Ahab is beginning to undergo a major psychological change. An intense reaction is developing within him against his own hybris. It almost always happens that an unconscious content which is approaching consciousness is first experienced in projection. So it is with Ahab. He is beginning to become aware of an intense revulsion for his own inflated state. If such a powerful affect became aware of its true object, it would probably result in self-destruction. In fact, the self-destructive tendency is already evident in the choice of the object for projection. The quadrant was a precious instrument aboard ship and to willfully break it indicates a self-destructive tendency at work. Sooner or later, the compensatory tendency of the unconscious becomes activated and destroys an erroneous or too one-sided conscious attitude. If the ego is completely identified with such an erroneous attitude, it will be destroyed with it, either by suicide or psychosis. The fiery reaction that bursts out of Ahab against the quadrant is the first manifestation of the rectifying energies which appear subsequently as the typhoon, the fire of the corpusants, and finally the white whale itself.

The Pequod now enters a violent typhoon, which means literally a great wind. It is also related to the Greek monster Typhon, traditionally associated with the Egyptian Set, the dismemberer of Osiris. Wind is a characteristic symbol of the spirit, the intangible energies of the transpersonal psyche. The etymologies of a multitude of words attest the equation, wind = spirit. The Yahweh of the Book of Job, one of whose manifestations was leviathan, appeared in the whirlwind. The typhoon thus symbolizes the activation of the impersonal, objective psyche which had been foreshadowed by Ahab's wild reaction against the quadrant. One of the first effects of the storm was to stave in Ahab's whale boat. Starbuck notes this fact and comments on it like a modern psychologist, "markest thou not that the gale comes from the eastward, the very course Ahab is to run for Moby-Dick? the very course he swung to this day noon? now mark his boat here; where is that stove? In the sternsheets, man; where he is wont to stand—his stand-point is stove, man!" (Chapter 119)

Ahab's standpoint is stove! Precisely. Starbuck's insight is brilliant, if only he could act on it. The same power that destroyed the quadrant for its hybris is destroying Ahab's standpoint. Two images for the same fact.

While the ship is being battered by the howling typhoon, that eerie phenomenon, St. Elmo's fire, appears. " 'Look aloft' cried Starbuck. 'The St. Elmo's Lights (corpus sancti) corpusants! the corpusants!' All the yard-arms were tipped with a pallid fire; and touched at each tri-pointed lightning-rod-end with three tapering white flames, each of the three tall masts was silently burning in that sulphurous air, like three gigantic wax tapers before an alter." (Chapter 119)

The ship has been transformed into a trinity of burning towers reminiscent of the golden doubloon with its triple mountain peaks, topped by a cock, a tower, and a flame. Preceded by the rushing wind of the typhoon, the Pequod's crew experience a pentecostal epiphany of the Holy Spirit. The original pentecostal fire is described in Acts 2.

When the day of Pentecost had come, they were all together in one place. And suddenly a sound came from heaven like the rush of a mighty wind, and it filled all the house where they were sitting. And there appeared to them tongues as of fire, distributed and resting on each one of them. And they were all filled with the Holy Spirit and began to speak in other tongues, as the Spirit gave them utterance.

Now there were dwelling in Jerusalem Jews, devout men from every nation under heaven. And at this sound the multitude came together, and they were bewildered, because each one heard them speaking in his own language. And they were amazed and wondered, saying, "Are not all these who are speaking Galileans? And how is it that we hear, each of us in his own native language?"

To understand the relation between Ahab's pentecostal fire and the Christian pentecost we must consider the latter's Old Testament "antitype."[4] This is the myth of the tower of Babel. At pentecost, the apostles received the gift of tongues, the capacity to communicate to those of all languages. In the earlier contrasting process, the tower of Babel resulted in a confusion of tongues, so every man spoke a different language. The two happenings are the reverse of each other. As described in Genesis, originally all men spoke one language, and they decided to build a tower:

"Come, let us build ourselves a city, and a tower with its top in the heavens, and let us make a name for ourselves lest we be scattered abroad upon the face of the whole earth."

And the Lord came down to see the city and the tower, which the sons of men had built. And the Lord said, "Behold, they are one people, and they have all one language; and this is only the beginning of what they will do; and nothing that they propose to do will now be impossible to them. Come, let us go down, and there confuse their language, that they may not understand one another's speech." (Genesis 11:4-7)

One of the tarot cards is entitled "The Tower." It pictures a tower being struck by lightning and broken apart. This picture refers to the tower of Babel, portraying the fire of God destroying the arrogant hybris of man. Another myth expressing the splitting, dissociating effects of the divine energy on man is found in Plato's myth of the original round man who, because of his hybris, is split in half by Zeus.[5]

[4] Alan Watts, *Myth and Ritual in Christianity* (New York: Thames and Hudson, 1953), p. 186.

[5] Plato, *Symposium*, pars. 189-92.

It is evident that the divine fire has different effects under different circumstances, i.e., at different stages of development. In the myth of the tower of Babel, all people have one language. This means that the original state of unconscious wholeness prevails; different aspects have not yet been separated by the process of conscious discrimination. This original wholeness is an inflated state, and leads to an inflated act—the building of the tower to challenge the power of God. Thus is evoked the divine response which breaks up or dismembers the original unconscious wholeness.

The myth of the pentecostal fire is the reverse of the foregoing. It occurs at a different stage of psychic development. Men are already broken up into different nationalities and speak different languages, signifying that different aspects of the personality have been differentiated by development but in the process have lost their relation to one another and to the original totality. Under these circumstances, the divine fire of the Holy Spirit comes as a unifying agency enabling the separated parts of the personality to communicate with one another and relate to their common center of totality.

Now which of these myths is applicable to Ahab and his crew? To ask the question is to answer it. Ahab is a tower-of-Babel-builder. And he has bent the whole crew to his purpose. They all speak the same language. The effect of the fire on the crew is a tendency to break up the unanimity of purpose. Stubb prays for mercy. Starbuck urges that the ship turn for home and a few chapters later contemplates killing Ahab. But although the dissociative tendency is present, it is not realized. Its actualization must wait for the next symbolic embodiment of the divine fire, the white whale Moby-Dick.

For the whole crew, the fire is a numinous experience. Ahab in particular is touched to the depths. It causes him to recollect previous incarnations:

> Oh! thou clear spirit of clear fire, whom on these seas I as Persian once did worship, till in the sacramental act so burned by thee, that to this hour I bear the scar; I now know thee, thou clear spirit, and I now know that thy right worship is defiance. To neither love nor reverence wilt thou be kind; and e'en for hate thou canst but kill; and all are killed. No fearless fool now fronts thee. I own thy speechless, placeless power; but to the last gasp of my earthquake life will dispute its unconditional, unintegral mastery in me. In the midst of the personi-

fied impersonal, a personality stands here. Though but a point at best; whencesoe'er I came; wheresoe'er I go; yet while I earthly live, the queenly personality lives in me, and feels her royal rights. But war is pain, and hate is woe. Come in thy lowest form of love, and I will kneel and kiss thee; but at thy highest, come as mere supernatural power; and though thou launches navies of full-freighted worlds, there's that in here that still remains indifferent. Oh, thou clear spirit, of thy fire thou madest me, and like a true child of fire, I breathe it back to thee. (Chapter 119)

Ahab recalls a previous incarnation, when he "as Persian once did worship." This sense of a timeless historical continuity transcending his immediate earthly existence is one of the manifestations of a deep activation of the collective unconscious. It is an archetypal idea that one can observe not uncommonly in the activation of the collective unconscious that accompanies psychosis. I recall, for instance, a schizophrenic patient who was inundated with archetypal images which made up the content of her hallucinations and delusions. She informed me that she could remember her previous incarnations for thousands of years. As is usual in such cases, she was most interested in talking about those incarnations when she had been a famous or important person.

Ahab's encounter with the fire finds its analogy in Job's encounter with Yahweh out of the whirlwind. The response and outcome are different, but the circumstances are similar. When Job meets the numinous experience of deity, his reply is, "I had heard of thee by the hearing of the ear, but now my eye sees thee; therefore I despise myself and repent in dust and ashes." (Job 42:5–6) Ahab's response is different. He says, "I own thy speechless, placeless power; but to the last gasp of my earthquake life will dispute its unconditional, unintegral mastery in me. In the midst of the personified impersonal, a personality stands here." These are brave and noble words, but are they true? Ahab is not a true personality. He is rather identified with an archetypal role which is living itself out through him. He himself is the personified impersonal and hence no personality. The question here is what conscious attitude will be taken toward the transpersonal energies of the psyche. Ahab has no attitude of his own toward the fire. If the sun insults him, he hits back; if fire is breathed to him, he breathes it back. This is no more than automatic reflex action—not the functioning of personality.

"Yet while I earthly live, the queenly personality lives in me, and feels her royal rights." The queen is the anima, that figure we have looked for in vain in *Moby-Dick*. Ahab is identified with the anima. We have already noted that for Ahab the anima has not been separated from the mother monster. Hence her manifestations, in identification with the ego, are primitive and undifferentiated. His moodiness and outbursts of affect are symptoms of anima possession.

In the midst of all this inflated ego-Self identity, there is also a glimpse of that calm, creative center of personality which partakes of the nature of deity and reminds us of the calm, generative center of the whale herd. "Though but a point at best . . . and though thou launchest navies of full-freighted worlds, there's that in here that still remains indifferent." Here is a hint of that "subtle body," the incorruptible philosophers' stone of the alchemists showing through Ahab's stormy ravings.

As Ahab proceeds in his soliloquy to the fire, another aspect emerges. The insight starts to dawn on him that God is incomplete and has his own grief. From this, it is only a short step to the realization that the transpersonal power needs human consciousness to realize itself.

> Oh! thou magnanimous! now do I glory in my genealogy. But thou art but my fiery father; my sweet mother, I know not. Oh, cruel! what hast thou done with her? There lies my puzzle; but thine is greater. Thou knowest not how came ye, hence callest thyself unbegotten; certainly knowest not thy beginning, hence callest thyself unbegun. I know that of me, which thou knowest not of thyself, oh, thou omnipotent. There is some unsuffusing thing beyond thee, thou clear spirit, to whom all thy eternity is but time, all thy creativeness mechanical. Through thee, thy flaming self, my scorched eyes do dimly see it. Oh, thou foundling fire, thou hermit immemorial, thou too hast thy incommunicable riddle, thy unparticipated grief. (Chapter 119)

Ahab is here very close to that awareness of the nature of deity which Jung considered Job to have acquired in his encounter with Yahweh. Job discovered "that Yahweh is not human but, in certain respects, less than human, that he is just what Yahweh says of leviathan." Yahweh's behavior was so intolerable from the human point of view because "it is the behavior of an unconscious being who cannot be judged morally. Yahweh is a phenomenon and, as

Job says, 'not a man.' "[6] In some respects God is less than man and needs his forbearance. In the passage above, Ahab seems close to this realization, but he does not quite reach it. Hence, the hunt for the white whale goes on.

The corpusants had a temporarily invigorating effect on Starbuck. We find him at least entertaining the idea of forcibly removing Ahab from command. He first considers killing Ahab, but realizes that is only because he has not the capacity to defy the living Ahab. "Make him a prisoner to be taken home? What! hope to wrest this old man's living power from his own living hands? Only a fool would try it. Say he were pinioned even; knotted all over with ropes and hawsers; chained down to ring-bolts on this cabin floor; he would be more hideous than a caged tiger, then. I could not endure the sight; could not possibly fly his howlings; all comfort, sleep itself, inestimable reason would leave me on the long intolerable voyage." (Chapter 123)

The proper course for Starbuck, the second in command, would be to depose the mad captain, but this is impossible for him to do. To Starbuck, Ahab is the effective figure of authority. Starbuck cannot find within himself an authority able to challenge that of Ahab. This means that Starbuck's inner authority is projected onto Ahab. In such a psychological situation, it would be futile, as Starbuck senses, to kill Ahab. The latter's authority would continue to live inside Starbuck and destroy him. As Starbuck says, "I stand alone here upon an open sea, with two oceans and a whole continent between me and the law." (Chapter 123) There is no outer, conventional law to support him. He is on his own and cannot find the inner power to act autonomously. Whole nations have fallen victim to criminal dictators for the same reason. Grown-up children never break the dependent bonds to the parents because they could not endure the wrath of frustrated tyranny or possessiveness. Like Starbuck, they are victims of the white whale by default.

[6] Jung, *Psychology and Religion*, par. 600.

16 *TRANSFORMATION*

DESPITE HIS IMMEDIATE reaction of defiance, subsequent events suggest that Ahab too was affected by the fire and storm. The first of these events was Ahab's new relationship to the crazy colored boy, Pip. A completely new aspect of Ahab's personality suddenly makes its appearance for the first time, namely, human feeling. Ahab finds a sailor mistreating Pip and suddenly, miraculously, a protective kindly reaction breaks out of Ahab. He goes to Pip's rescue, crying "Hands off from that holiness." And then he decides to share his cabin with Pip. "There can be no hearts above the snow-line. Oh, ye frozen heavens! look down here. Ye did beget this luckless child, and have abandoned him, ye creative libertines. Here, boy; Ahab's cabin shall be Pip's home henceforth, while Ahab lives. Thou touchest my inmost centre, boy; thou art tied to me by cords woven of my heart-strings. Come, let's down." (Chapter 125)

Ahab has indeed been touched by Job's lesson. If the impersonal energies of life are only phenomena without feeling or consciousness, all the more reason for conscious man to affirm human values. Perhaps man can give even God a lesson in morality: "Lo! ye believers in gods all goodness, and in man all ill, lo you! see the omniscient gods oblivious of suffering man; and man, though idiotic, and knowing not what he does, yet full of the sweet things of love and gratitude. Come! I feel prouder leading thee by thy black hand, than though I grasped an Emperor's!" (Chapter 125)

Is this Ahab speaking? Expressing pride at having feelings of love and gratitude? This is not the Ahab we know. A radical change is occurring within him. Here is the decisive turning point in *Moby-Dick*. Ahab has experienced a profound transformation. Although the hunt continues and leads inexorably to its tragic end, it is henceforth experienced by a feeling human being, not a heartless madman. Ahab, although he dies, is healed. The voyage has been worth it after all. Up to this point, we have had many reasons for grave concern regarding Melville's personal fate. We now have reason for reassurance. Although the dangers were most serious, the daring resolve to create out of his hatred has been justified. The pact with the devil has been survived. Of course, no such sudden realization came to Melville when he reached this point in the writing of *Moby-Dick*. The whole symbolic drama of Ahab's, like a crucial dream, prefigures a course of events that would take years, perhaps a lifetime to be consciously realized. Much later in life, in a poem, Melville could write, "Healed of my hurt, I laud the inhuman sea."[1] But this is after the fact. It is quite another thing, in the midst of the hell-fire of *Moby-Dick*, to suddenly come upon the promise of a healing yet to come.

Pip is Ahab's shadow, his opposite half. Together they make a whole. As the old Manxman put it, "One daft with strength, the other daft with weakness." The fact that Ahab is able to relate feelingly to Pip means that he is at last approaching an acceptance of his own weak side and even finding value in it.

Soon Ahab is able to say to Pip, "I do suck most wondrous philosophies from thee! Some unknown worlds must empty into thee" (Chapter 127). Ahab discovers the conscious acceptance of one's weak, inferior side opens up new worlds of experience and enlarges the personality. All human relationship is based on the fact of human weakness. Those who are not aware of their own weakness are tyrants or madmen like Ahab. Strength and weakness are a pair of opposites, and from the broad viewpoint one is no more valuable than the other. Each has its own particular virtue, and each if carried to extremes can turn into its opposite. The relationship between Ahab and Pip thus represents a reconciliation of opposites, which is one of the features of the integrated personality. As Olson points out, his relation to Pip brings about a permanent change in Ahab.

> Though Ahab continues to curse the gods for their "inhumanities," his tone, from this moment is richer, quieter, less angry and strident. He even questions his former blasphemies, for a bottomed sadness grows in him as Pip lives in the cabin with him. . . . What Pip wrought in Ahab throws over the end of *Moby-Dick* a veil of grief, relaxes the tensions of its hate, and permits a sympathy for the stricken man that Ahab's insistent diabolism up to the storm would not have evoked. The end of this fire-forked tragedy is enriched by a pity in the very jaws of terror.[2]

---

[1] "Pebbles," *Collected Poems*, p. 206.
[2] Olson, *op. cit.*, pp. 60ff.

Very soon after the emergence of Ahab's love for Pip, the Pequod meets the whaleship Rachel. The son of the Rachel's captain is missing in a lost whaleboat and the captain begs Ahab to help in the search. Ahab refuses but with genuine regrets as indicated by his parting words, "God bless ye, man, and may I forgive myself, but I must go." This ship named Rachel looking for its lost child associates to the prophecy in the thirty-first chapter of Jeremiah, which promises the Jews return from exile. This passage is also quoted in Matthew (2:18) as referring to the coming of Christ and Herod's slaughter of the innocents following the birth of Jesus.

> A voice is heard in Ramah,
> lamentation and bitter weeping.
> Rachel is weeping for her children;
> she refuses to be comforted for
> her children,
> because they are not.
> Thus says the Lord:
> Keep your voice from weeping,
> and your eyes from tears;
> for your work shall be rewarded
> Says the Lord,
> And they shall come back from
> the land of the enemy.
> There is hope for your future, says the Lord
> (Jer. 31:15–17)

It is no accident that the sad ship is encountered almost immediately after Ahab begins to realize his love for Pip. Rachel was one of the ancestral mothers of the Jews. Hence, she is a representative figure of the positive archetypal mother, and the appearance of a ship bearing her name indicates the activation of this archetype. In the midst of the storm Ahab had shouted to the fire, "Thou art but my fiery father; my sweet mother I know not. Oh, cruel! What hast thou done with her? There lies my puzzle." (Chapter 119) The "sweet mother," the positive aspect of the mother archetype, is beginning to make its appearance in the ship Rachel. Just as Pip's sanity was lost overboard, the Rachel has lost the son of the captain. Perhaps significantly, the lost son was twelve years old, the same age as Melville when his father had a mental breakdown and died. Although Ahab did not respond to the pleas of the Rachel, the very fact that the compassionate ship enters the story at this point is significant. It means that a positive feminine, feeling element has entered the situation. It is this ship and what it symbolizes that is later the agent of salvation for Ishmael.

Finally in Chapter 132, titled "The Symphony," the demonisms are stripped away entirely and Ahab is revealed to himself and to us in his full humanity. The meaning of his love for Pip and the meeting of the Rachel become manifest in Ahab's consciousness,

> the lovely aromas in that enchanted air did at last seem to dispel, for a moment, the cankerous thing in his soul. That glad, happy air, that winsome sky, did at last stroke and caress him; the stepmother world, so long cruel—forbidding—now threw affectionate arms round his stubborn neck, and did seem to joyously sob over him, as if over one that however wilful and erring, she could yet find it in her heart to save and to bless. From beneath his slouched hat Ahab dropped a tear into the sea; nor did all the Pacific contain such wealth as that one wee drop.
>
> "Oh, Starbuck! it is a mild, mild wind, and a mild looking sky. On such a day—very much such a sweetness as this—I struck my first whale—a boy-harpooner of eighteen! Forty—forty—forty years ago! Forty years of continual whaling! forty years of privation, and peril, and storm-time! forty years on the pitiless sea! for forty years has Ahab forsaken the peaceful land, for forty years to make war on the horrors of the deep! Aye and yes, Starbuck, out of those forty years I have not spent three ashore. When I think of this life I have led; the desolation of solitude it has been; the masoned, walled-town of a Captain's exclusiveness, which admits but small entrance to any sympathy from the green country without—oh, weariness! heaviness! Guinea-coast slavery of solitary command!—When I think of all this; only half-suspected, not so keenly known to me before—and how for forty years I have fed upon dry salted fare—fit emblem of the dry nourishment of my soul!—when the poorest landsman has had fresh fruit to his daily hand, and broken the world's fresh bread to my mouldy crusts—away, whole oceans away, from that young girl-wife I wedded past fifty, and sailed for Cape Horn the next day, leaving her one dent in my marriage pillow—wife? wife?—rather a widow with her husband alive! Aye, I widowed that poor girl when I married her, Starbuck; and then, the madness, the frenzy, the boiling blood and the smoking brow, with which, for a thousand lowerings old Ahab has furiously, foamingly chased his prey—more a demon than a man!—aye, aye! what a forty years' fool—fool—old fool, has old Ahab been! . . . . I feel

deadly faint, bowed and humped, as though I were Adam, staggering beneath the piled centuries since Paradise. God! God!—crack my heart—stave my brain!"

In this stunning passage, we finally meet Ahab as a full human being. Now we see his life in a larger perspective. A new level of consciousness has dawned on Ahab. He now realizes the compulsive, demonic nature of his previous state, and, for the present at least, is released from it. The missing anima appears, Ahab's wife, and feeling for her transforms the situation. This point marks the climax of *Moby-Dick*. Ahab's hate has spent itself, and in its place comes sorrow for his folly. Now Ahab can contemplate with Shakespeare, how ". . . strange it is that nature must compel us to lament our most persisted deeds."[3]

Throughout this climactic passage, the number forty appears again and again. It is repeated a total of eleven times. This is an important clue. It is as though Melville were shouting at us, forcing us to bring up associations to the number forty. What are these associations? Forty is reminiscent of Noah's flood. "And rain fell upon the earth forty days and forty nights." (Gen. 7:12) Also, Moses met Yahweh in a cloud on Mount Sinai, "And Moses entered the cloud, and went up on the mountain. And Moses was on the mountain forty days and forty nights." (Exod. 24:18) After the Jews left Egypt and before they reached Canaan, they wandered in the wilderness for forty years. "And the Lord's anger was kindled against Israel, and he made them wander in the wilderness forty years, until all the generation that had done evil in the sight of the Lord was consumed." (Num. 32:13) The number forty also associates to the temptation of Jesus. "And Jesus, full of the Holy Spirit, returned from the Jordan, and was led by the Spirit for forty days in the wilderness, tempted by the Devil." (Luke 4:1,2)

These associations connect the number forty with a manifestation of deity. With only one exception (Moses meeting Yahweh on Sinai) they refer to vengeful, destructive, or tempting acts of God which endanger man.

Another set of associations to forty carries a somewhat different significance. It is forty days between Easter and ascension, referring to the intermediate period between two states of being. Similarly,

[3] *Antony and Cleopatra*, IV, i.

according to Genesis 50:3, forty days was the period required for Egyptian embalming. In alchemical symbolism, the *nigredo* phase or blackening usually took forty days.[4] According to Jung, forty is a prefiguration of the whole alchemical opus.[5]

We thus have two sets of associations to the number forty. One relates it to the active intervention of deity into the affairs of man, which may have destructive or dangerous consequences. The other set of associations relates the number forty to a transition or transformation process which leads from one state of being to another. Actually, these two are different aspects of the same thing. The flood, the Jews in the wilderness, and the temptation of Jesus are also transition processes leading from one state to a new one.

Applying these mythical images to the psychology of the individual, we can say that Ahab's forty years at sea symbolizes the encounter of the conscious ego with the transpersonal psyche. This has major transformative potentialities, but initially the encounter is experienced as destructive, wounding, and alienating. The growth and transformation of consciousness can occur only when the ego's inflated state of identification with the Self has been broken down. And this can happen only through a "wilderness" or *nigredo* experience.

In this moment of sanity, Ahab, like Moses, sees the promised land that he is not permitted to enter. In his cry, "God! God!— crack my heart—stave my brain!" he is asking for release. He is freely seeking the consequences of the attitude he now renounces. He accepts his Osirian fate of dismemberment. This is why he can not accept Starbuck's suggestion to turn about and head for home. Ahab has been carrying the impossible burden of an identification with the collective unconscious, "staggering beneath the piled centuries." He can be released from that burden only by meeting the consequences of carrying it. As the life of Jesus shows, it is a fearful thing to live out a myth. Ahab must meet his fate, but now he can do it consciously as a feeling human being. His story can now fulfill Aristotle's requirements for true tragedy. No longer mad, he can evoke pity as well as terror.

In another passage, Ahab shows that he is finally beginning to

---

[4] Jung, *Mysterium Coniunctionis*, par. 729.
[5] Ibid., par. 77, n. 215.

distinguish between himself, the ego, and the archetypal energies that work through him.

> What is it, what nameless, inscrutable, unearthly thing is it; what cozzening, hidden lord and master, and cruel, remorseless emperor commands me; that against all natural lovings and longings, I so keep pushing, and crowding, and jamming myself on all the time; recklessly making me ready to do what in my own proper, natural heart, I durst not so much as dare? Is Ahab, Ahab? Is it I, God, or who, that lifts this arm? But if the great sun move not of himself; but is as an errand-boy in heaven; nor one single star can revolve, but by some invisible power; how then can this one small heart beat; this one small brain think thoughts; unless God does that beating, does that thinking, does that living, and not I. By heaven, man, we are turned round and round in this world, like yonder windlass, and Fate is the handspike. (Chapter 132)

Fate is everything that happens as a result of unconscious dynamisms. To the extent that one is conscious, fate is changed into choice. Ahab is beginning to realize this. The identity between ego and Self is breaking up.

17 DEATH AND REBIRTH

AT LAST the white whale is sighted, and the final act of the tragedy begins. For three days Moby-Dick is chased. Harpoon in hand, Ahab meets him for three successive encounters. The symbolism of the three-day hunt and the triple encounter is significant. It is an archetypal motif referring to the fulfillment of a development process in time. It signifies the completion, for good or ill, of a fateful destiny. In fairy tales, we frequently encounter the theme of the crucial act which must be repeated three times. The Greek mythical symbol for destiny, the three Fates, has a threefold nature: Clotho who spins the thread of life, Lachesis who measures it, and Atropos who cuts it. In Teutonic myth, there are three Norns: Urd, Verdandi, and Shuld. Urd, the aged one, refers to the past, Verdandi to the present, and Shuld to the future. There seems to be a deep-seated archetypal tendency to organize temporal or developmental events in terms of a threefold pattern. Starbuck expresses this instinctive knowledge as he is contemplating the beginning of the third day of the chase. "And this the critical third day?—For when three days flow together in one continuous intense pursuit; be sure the first is the morning, the second the noon, and the third the evening and the end of that thing—be that end what it may." (Chapter 135)

Another facet of this same symbolical fact is the relation between the number three and the theme of "the night sea journey." This latter image is a symbol of death and rebirth, i.e., a psychological transformation. Typically, in the legends of the hero swallowed by the monster, the hero spends three days in the belly of the monster, e.g., Jonah was in the belly of the whale for "three days and three nights." Three days elapsed between Jesus' death and his resurrection. The crucifixion itself was a triple one, since Jesus was crucified between two thieves. These mythological parallels indicate that Ahab's encounter with the white whale is following the typical pattern of death and rebirth.

Another significant image comes up twice in these final pages—the image of spiral motion. On the first day of the chase, after the whale had wrecked Ahab's boat: "Moby-Dick swam swiftly round and round the wrecked crew. . . . so revolvingly appalling was the White Whale's aspect, and so planetarily swift the ever-contracting circles he made, that he seemed horizontally swooping upon them." (Chapter 133)

The same image appears more powerfully in the very final scene as the Pequod is sinking beneath the waves.

> So, floating on the margin of the ensuing scene, and in full sight of it, when the half-spent suction of the sunk ship reached me, I was then, but slowly, drawn towards the closing vortex. When I reached it, it had subsided to a creamy pool. Round and round, then, and ever contracting towards the buttonlike black bubble at the axis of that slowly wheeling circle, like another Ixion I did revolve. Till, gaining that vital centre, the black bubble upward burst; and now, liberated by reason of its cunning spring, and, owing to its great buoyancy, rising with great force, the coffin life-buoy shot lengthwise from the sea, fell over, and floated by my side. (Epilogue)

The white whale and its effects are thus twice associated with the image of spiral motion. The spiral is a very ancient symbol. One finds it, for instance, on Mycenaean artifacts, c. 1500 B.C. The Kundalini serpent of Tantric Yoga is coiled in a spiral of three and one-half turns around a creative central point. Yahweh appeared to Job out of the spiral whirlwind. A spiral is basically a circular movement toward or away from a central point or axis. Hence, it is an apt symbol for the process of individuation, which is a kind of circumambulation in ever smaller circles of the Self. Where this unconscious dynamism that seeks the center is activated without the ego's being consciously related to it, dangerous or destructive aspects of spiral form appear. The image of the whirlpool in which Ishmael revolves belongs to this latter category. The whirlpool symbolizes, as it were, the involuntary individuation process that seeks the central Self in disregard of the conscious ego. If the latter is too weak and immature to relate to this central dynamism, it will be sucked down and destroyed.

Melville provides us with another interesting association to the whirlpool. He says that Ishmael went round and round the whirlpool "like another Ixion." Ixion is a figure in Greek myth who offended Zeus by attempting to seduce Hera. In punishment for this act of hybris, Zeus had Ixion bound to a fiery wheel which revolved eternally. The wheel is a mandala, a symbol of the Self. Ixion, by presuming to seduce a goddess, was acting out of an inflated attitude. He was identified with the Self and hence behaved as though he were a deity. In such a state, the Self becomes a fiery torture wheel to the ego. The individual is bound to it by his own identification. This false and unconscious relation of the ego to the divine, suprapersonal energies of the psyche causes them to become a fiery torment. A parallel image is found in the Indian myth of the wheel of rebirth. This wheel is rotated by the three animals the pig, the cock, and the snake, symbols of instinctive desirousness. According to the myth, as long as a man is bound to this torture wheel he must endure repeated reincarnations. He is released only by the enlightenment (Consciousness) which separates him from identification with his desires.

Ahab was an Ixion. His hybris, deriving from an identification with the Self, bound him to its fiery wheel. We have had occasion to note the intolerable burden he complained of carrying. The white whale and the whirlpool it creates are one. Moby-Dick is the fiery wheel of torment to which Ahab was bound by his inflated identification with deity. Ahab expresses this fiery bondage in his final words just before the rope catches him around the neck and carries him into the sea, tied to the whale by his own harpoon line.

Oh, lonely death in lonely life? Oh, now I feel my topmost greatness lies in my topmost grief. Ho, Ho! from all your furthest bounds, pour ye now in, ye bold billows of my whole foregone life, and top this one piled comber of my death! Towards thee I roll, thou all-destroying but unconquering whale; to the last I grapple with thee; from hell's heart I stab at thee; for hate's sake I spit my last breath at thee. Sink all coffins and all hearses to one common pool! and since neither can be mine, let me then tow to pieces, while still chasing thee, though tied to thee, thou damned whale! *Thus*, I give up the spear! (Chapter 135)

Ahab's dying words are, "*Thus*, I give up the spear!" And thus, he also gives up the ghost. From his first encounter with the whale, Ahab had been carrying a spear of vengeance against him. And now, in the finale, he gives up that spear. The spell is broken, vengeance has died, and the drama is done.

Our last view of Ahab is to see him being carried into the depths of the sea, tied to Moby-Dick by his harpoon line. This image recalls the monkey rope which was the connecting cord between Ishmael and Queequeg; it reminds us of Ahab's remark to Pip, "Thou touchest my inmost centre, boy; thou art tied to me by cords woven of my heart strings"; and also it is reminiscent of what was seen at the calm center of the whale mandala. "As when the stricken whale, that from the tub has reeled out hundreds of fathoms of rope; as after deep sounding, he floats up again, and shows the slackened curling line buoyantly rising and spiralling towards the air; so now, Starbuck saw long coils of the umbilical cord of Madame Leviathan, by which the young cub seemed still tethered to its dam." (Chapter 87)

Harpoon line and umbilical cord are equated. Thus, Ahab in his death has reconnected himself with the whale as Great Mother. Beneath his compulsive hatred and fury, this has been the hidden intent all along. Now it is fulfilled. In Ahab's death, the white whale and its antagonist are reunited. A version of the *coniunctio* that reconciles the opposites has occurred. And out of this union comes the possibility of rebirth.

There is a survivor. Queequeg's coffin was ejected from the very center of the whirlpool's vortex. The coffin-lifebuoy shot length-wise from the sea, floated by Ishmael's side, and saved him from otherwise certain death. This coffin had been made at the request of Queequeg when he was close to death with fever. It had been made to his exact measurements, and later Queequeg made it still more his own by pouring lavishly his time and energy into carving it. "Many spare hours he spent, in carving the lid with all manner of grotesque figures and drawings; and it seemed that hereby he was striving, in his rude way, to copy parts of the twisted tattooing on his body. And this tattooing, had been the work of a departed prophet and seer of his island, who, by those hieroglyphic marks, had written out on his body a complete theory of the heavens and the earth, and a mystical treatise on the art of attaining truth." (Chapter 110)

Queequeg's coffin thus became a symbolic duplicate of himself— at least that part of himself that carried the eternal primal signs and mysteries of being. The carved coffin is a representation of the saving wisdom of the primordial psyche. A coffin is one of the aspects of the Great Mother archetype. As a protective container, it is analogous to cradle and womb. Queequeg's coffin-lifebuoy carries the paradoxical meaning of both the container of death and the womb of rebirth. The double significance of the coffin had occurred to Ahab. When Queequeg recovered and the coffin was not needed, it was caulked and made into a lifebuoy. Ahab mused over that strange object, a coffin-lifebuoy. "A lifebuoy of a coffin! Does it go further? Can it be that in some spiritual sense the coffin is, after all, but an immortality preserver! I'll think of that. But no. So far gone am I in the dark side of earth, that its other side, the theoretic bright one, seems but uncertain twilight to me." (Chapter 127)

The same whirlpool wheel of the Self which sucked the ill-fated Pequod down to death, threw up out of its center the protective vessel of rebirth for Ishmael. In this final scene, Queequeg's redemptive function for Ishmael, which was noted earlier, is verified. Ishmael's words shortly after meeting Queequeg came back to us with added meaning: "I felt a melting in me. No more my splintered heart and maddened hand were turned against the wolfish world. This soothing savage had redeemed it." (Chapter 10)

The epilogue on the final page is headed by a quotation from Job. "And I only am escaped alone to tell thee." This phrase comes at the very beginning of the story of Job, when he is informed of the catastrophes that have befallen him. Consciously or unconsciously, Melville is giving us a clear statement that the reading of *Moby-*

Dick should be followed by the reading of Job. It is to that latter source we must go to find the reconciliation between God and man that *Moby-Dick* hints at but does not achieve.

In 1819, the year of Melville's birth, the whaleship Essex sailed from Nantucket for the Pacific cruising grounds. A little over a year later, this ship was deliberately rammed twice by a sperm whale and sank within ten minutes. The crew set out in three whale boats for the coast of South America, two thousand miles away. After the most frightful privations which reduced the survivors to cannibalism, eight of the original twenty men were finally rescued. Owen Chase, the first mate of the Essex, wrote a narrative of his experiences, which was read by Melville and profoundly affected him. In Chapter 45 of *Moby-Dick*, the tragedy of the Essex is described. Melville records in notes written in his copy of Chase's book how he first heard the story of the Essex. During Melville's whaling voyage, they met another Nantucket ship and spoke with her. "In the forecastle I made the acquaintance of a fine lad of sixteen or thereabouts, a son of Owen Chase. I questioned him concerning his father's adventure; . . . he went to his chest and handed me a copy of the narrative. . . . The reading of this wondrous story upon the landless sea, and close to the very latitude of the shipwreck had a surprising effect on me."[6]

The "surprising effect" indicates that the Essex story touched a complex or unconscious issue in Melville. *Moby-Dick* can be taken as the working out of that complex. Every complex has an archetypal core. In this case, the core is the Job archetype, man's encounter with an apparently malevolent deity. In psychological terms, it is the ego's experience of being wounded by encounter with the Self. Resentment and lust for vengeance are symptoms of the wound.

The ego, having separated itself from its unconscious matrix and from nature, is wounded to discover its alienated state. The wound exists prior to its discovery, in fact it occurs at the birth of the ego. The anguished realization of one's wounded condition is actually the first step toward recovery of the lost wholeness. Resentment of the injury can contain the seeds of a future religious attitude. Hatred of God at least grants His existence. It assumes a responsible trans-

---

[6] Melville quoted in Owen Chase, *Shipwreck of the Whaleship Essex* (New York: Corinth Books, 1963), p. 138.

personal agency to whom one can bring his grievances, or even against whom one may retaliate. The crucial feature is the ego's awareness of the "other," the basic requirement for dialogue.

Ahab's mad pursuit of the whale is a kind of primitive, negative dialogue with the Self. His persistence, like Job's, leads him eventually to the corrective experience which teaches the ego, decisively, the difference between it and the Self. From such a defeat, consciously lived, comes the redeeming encounter with the *numinosum*. Jung says, *"the experience of the self is always a defeat for the ego."*[7] This is the message of Job, and this is the lesson of *Moby-Dick*.

Like Ishmael, Melville barely survived the writing of *Moby-Dick*. In fact, it is likely that the images of Ahab and the white whale, like Moses' brazen serpent, were instruments of his own ultimate healing. The excruciating conflict between the opposites which Melville endured was finally reconciled. Eventually, he experienced the *coniunctio* that was prefigured at the end of *Moby-Dick*. In *Clarel*, written many years later, he says,

> Speak not evil of the evil:
> Evil and good they braided play
> Into one cord.[8]

And in a late poem he wrote:

> Healed of my hurt, I laud the inhuman sea—
> Yea, bless the Angels Four that there convene;
> For healed I am even by their pitiless breath
> Distilled in wholesome dew named rosemarine.[9]

---

[7] Jung, *Mysterium Coniunctionis*, par. 778.
[8] *Clarel*, p. 419.
[9] "Pebbles," *Collected Poems*, p. 206.

BIBLIOGRAPHY

The American Heritage Book of Indians. Edited by William Brandon. Simon and Schuster. New York, 1961.

Arvin, Newton. *Herman Melville*. William Sloane Associates. New York, 1950.

Bishop, Jim. *The Day Lincoln was Shot*. Harper & Brothers. New York, 1955.

Bowen, Merlin. *The Long Encounter*. University of Chicago Press, Chicago, 1960.

Braswell, William. *Melville's Religious Thought*. Pageant Books. New York, 1959.

Campbell, Joseph. *The Masks of God: Primitive Mythology*. Viking Press. New York, 1959.

Chase, Owen. *Shipwreck of the Whaleship Essex*. Corinth Books. New York, 1963.

Dante. *The Divine Comedy*. Translated by Lawrence Grant White. Pantheon Books. New York, 1948.

Dickinson, Emily. *The Complete Poems of Emily Dickinson*. Edited by Thomas H. Johnson. Little, Brown and Co. Boston and Toronto, 1960.

Edinger, Edward F. *Ego and Archetype*. G. P. Putnam's Sons. New York, 1972.

Eliade, Mircea. *Images and Symbols*. Sheed & Ward. New York, 1961.

Emerson, Ralph Waldo. *The Writings of Ralph Waldo Emerson*. Modern Library. Random House. New York, 1940.

Finkelstein, Dorothee Metlitsky. *Melville's Orienda*. Yale University Press. New Haven and London, 1961.

Franklin, H. Bruce. *The Wake of the Gods*. Stanford University Press. Stanford, 1963.

Frost, Robert. *Complete Poems of Robert Frost*. Holt, Rinehart & Winston, New York, 1962.

Ginzberg, L. *Legends of the Bible*. Simon and Schuster. New York, 1956.

Goddard, Harold C. *The Meaning of Shakespeare*. University of Chicago Press. Chicago, 1951.

Goethe. *Faust.* Translated by Louis MacNeice. Oxford University Press. Galaxy Books. New York, 1960.

Goethe. *Faust.* Translated by G. M. Priest. Knopf. New York, 1963.

Harding, M. Esther. *Psychic Energy: Its Source and Transformation.* Princeton University Press. Princeton, 1973.

Homer. *Odyssey.* Translated by A. T. Murray. Loeb Classical Library. Harvard University Press. Cambridge and London, 1960.

James, William. *The Varieties of Religious Experience.* Modern Library. Random House. New York, n.d.

Jonas, Hans. *The Gnostic Religion.* Beacon Press. Boston, 1958.

Jung, C. G. *Collected Works.* (CW) Princeton University Press. Princeton, various dates:

> *Symbols of Transformation.* CW Volume 5.
>
> *The Structure and Dynamics of the Psyche.* CW Volume 8.
>
> *The Archetypes and the Collective Unconscious.* CW Volume 9i.
>
> *Psychology and Religion: West and East.* CW Volume 11.
>
> *Psychology and Alchemy.* CW Volume 12.
>
> *Alchemical Studies.* CW Volume 13.
>
> *Mysterium Coniunctionis.* CW Volume 14.
>
> *The Spirit in Man, Art, and Literature.* CW Volume 15.
>
> *The Development of Personality.* CW Volume 17.

Jung, C. G. *Memories, Dreams, Reflections.* Pantheon Books. New York, 1963.

Kirsch, James. "The Enigma of Moby Dick." *Journal of Analytical Psychology.* Volume III, Number 2. July 1958.

Kirsch, James. "The Problem of Dictatorship as Represented in Moby Dick." *Current Trends in Analytical Psychology.* Tavistock. London, 1961.

Leyda, Jay. *The Melville Log.* Harcourt Brace & Co. New York, 1951.

Melville, Herman.

> *Typee.* (1846) Various editions.
>
> *Omoo.* (1847)   "   "
>
> *Mardi.* (1849)   "   "
>
> *Redburn.* (1849)   "   "
>
> *White Jacket.*
>
> (1850)   "   "
>
> *Moby-Dick* (1851) Best edition, Hendricks House. New York, 1962, with exhaustive notes by Luther S. Mansfield and Howard P. Vincent.
>
> *Pierre, or the Ambiguities.* (1852) Best edition, Hendricks House.

New York, 1962, with excellent, lengthy psychological introduction by Henry A. Murray.

Clarel. (1876) Hendricks House. New York, 1960.

Collected Poems (1849–1891). Edited by Howard P. Vincent. Packard and Company. Hendricks House. Chicago, 1947.

Metcalf, Eleanor. *Herman Melville.* Harvard University Press. Cambridge, 1953.

Murray, Henry A. "In Nomine Diaboli." *Moby-Dick Centennial Essays.* Southern Methodist University Press. Dallas, 1953.

Neumann, Erich. *The Origins and History of Consciousness.* Bollingen Series XLII. Pantheon Books. New York, 1954.

Olson, Charles. *Call Me Ishmael.* Grove Press. New York, 1947.

Onians, R. B. *The Origins of European Thought.* Cambridge University Press. Cambridge, 1951.

Otto, Rudolf. *The Idea of the Holy.* Oxford University Press. London, 1950.

Pops, Martin Leonard. *The Melville Archetype.* The Kent State University Press. Kent, Ohio, 1970.

Slotkin, Richard. *Regeneration Through Violence: The Mythology of the American Frontier, 1600–1860.* Wesleyan University Press. Middletown, Conn., 1973.

Sweeney, Gerard M. *Melville's Use of Classical Mythology.* Rodopi N.V. Amsterdam, 1975.

Wright, Nathalia. *Melville's Use of the Bible.* Reprinted by Octagon Books. New York, 1974.

Thompson, Lawrance. *Melville's Quarrel with God.* Princeton University Press. Princeton, 1952.

Todd, Harriet A. *The Quest in the Works of Herman Melville.* Privately printed. 1961.

Watts, Alan. *Myth and Ritual in Christianity.* Thames and Hudson. London and New York, 1953.

GLOSSARY

AMPLIFICATION. A method of dream interpretation developed by Jung in which a dream image or motif is enlarged, clarified, and given a meaningful context by comparing it with similar images from mythology, folklore, and comparative religion. Amplification establishes the collective context of a dream, enabling it to be seen, not only in its personal aspect, but also in general archetypal terms which are common to all humanity.

ANIMA. Latin, "soul." The unconscious, feminine side of a man's personality. She is personified in dreams by images of women ranging in nature from harlot and seductress to divine Wisdom and spiritual guide. Identification with the anima causes a man to become effeminate, sulky, and resentful. Projection of the anima accounts for a man's falling in love.

ANIMUS. Latin, masc. "soul." The unconscious masculine side of a woman's personality. He is the logos spirit principle in women. When identified with the animus a woman becomes argumentative and rigidly opinionated. Projection of the animus leads to a woman's falling in love.

ARCHETYPE, ARCHETYPAL IMAGE. A universal and recurring image, pattern, or motif representing a typical human experience. Archetypal images come from the collective unconscious and are the basic contents of religions, mythologies, legends, and fairy tales. They also emerge from the collective unconscious in individuals through dreams and visions. Encounter with an archetypal image evokes a strong emotional reaction, conveying a sense of divine or transpersonal power which transcends the ego.

ASSOCIATION. The spontaneous flow of interconnected thoughts and images following from a specific idea. Associations are determined by unconscious, meaningful connections and are never fortuitous.

COLLECTIVE UNCONSCIOUS. The deepest layer of the unconscious, which is ordinarily inaccessible to awareness. Its nature is suprapersonal, universal, and nonindividual. Its manifestations are experienced as alien to the ego, numinous, or divine. The contents of the collective unconscious are the archetypes and their specific symbolic representations, archetypal images (*q.v.*).

COMPLEX. An emotionally charged unconscious entity composed of a number of associated ideas grouped around a central core which is an archetypal image..One recognizes that a complex has been activated when emotion upsets psychic balance and disturbs the customary function of the ego.

CONIUNCTIO. A term from alchemy referring to the archetypal image of the sacred marriage or union of opposites. It signifies the goal of individuation, the conscious realization of the Self.

EGO. The center of consciousness and the seat of the individual's experience of subjective identity.

EXTRAVERSION. A mode of psychic functioning in which interest, value, and meaning are attached primarily to external objects. Inner subjective matters are given little worth. Opposite of introversion.

FEELING. One of the four psychic functions according to Jung. It is the rational (i.e., judgmental) function that determines value and promotes personal relationship.

FUNCTION, INFERIOR. That psychological function least developed in a particular individual. It expresses itself in primitive, archaic and affect-laden ways. The inferior function is the gateway to the collective unconscious.

FUNCTIONS, PSYCHOLOGICAL. There are four modes of psychic adaptation according to Jung: thinking, feeling, sensation, and intuition. See each.

FUNCTION, SUPERIOR. The most highly developed and differentiated of the psychological functions in a particular individual.

INDIVIDUATION. The conscious realization and fulfillment of one's unique being. It is associated with typical archetypal imagery and leads to the experiencing of the Self as the center of personality transcending the ego. It begins with one or more decisive experiences challenging ego-centricity and producing the awareness that the ego is subordinate to a more comprehensive psychic entity.

INFLATION. A psychic state characterized by an exaggerated and unreal sense of one's own importance. It is caused by an identification of the ego with an archetypal image.

INTROVERSION. A mode of psychic functioning in which interest, value, and meaning are found predominantly in the inner life of the individual. Values are determined largely by the subject's internal reactions. Opposite of extraversion.

INTUITION. One of the four psychic functions according to Jung. It is perception via the unconscious, i.e., perception of contents or conclusions whose origin is obscure.

LIBIDO. The psychic energy that motivates the psyche. Interest, attention, and drive are all expressions of libido. The libido invested in a given item is indicated by the quantity of its "value-charge," either positive or negative.

MANDALA. Sanskrit, "magic circle." In analytical psychology, an archetypal image representing the Self. The basic mandala is a circle with a square or other fourfold structure superimposed. Mandalas are found in the culture-products of all races. They seem to represent a central integrating principle which lies at the root of the psyche.

NEKYIA. A term borrowed from Homer's *Odyssey* signifying a descent to the underworld, i.e., an encounter with the collective unconscious.

NUMINOSUM, NUMINOUS. First used by Rudolf Otto to describe the experience of the divine as awesome, terrifying, and "wholly other." In analytical psychology, it is used to describe the ego's experience of an archetype, especially the Self.

OBJECTIVE PSYCHE. See collective unconscious.

PARTICIPATION MYSTIQUE. A condition of magical, unconscious identity between the ego and the collective unconscious and the outer world.

PERSONA. Latin, "actor's mask." It is the partially calculated public face an individual assumes in relating to others. The persona is derived from the expectations of society and the early training by parents and teachers. It is the role one plays in society.

PROJECTION. The process whereby an unconscious quality or content of one's own is perceived and reacted to in an outer object.

QUATERNITY. The archetype of fourfoldness symbolizing wholeness. It is closely associated with representations of the Self.

SELF. The central and comprehensive archetype expressing the totality of the psyche as organized around a dynamic center. It is commonly symbolized by a mandala or a paradoxical union of opposites. The Self is experienced as the objective, transpersonal center of identity which transcends the ego. Empirically it cannot be distinguished from the image of God.

SENSATION. One of the four psychic functions according to Jung. It is that function which perceives and adapts to external reality via the senses.

SHADOW. An unconscious part of the personality usually containing inferior characteristics and weaknesses which the individual's self-esteem will not permit him to recognize as his own. It is the first layer of the unconscious to be encountered in psychological analysis and is personified in dreams by dark and dubious figures of the same sex as the dreamer.

SYNCHRONICITY. A term coined by Jung for a postulated acausal connecting principle to explain the occurrence of meaningful coincidence, i.e., whenever an inner psychic happening (dream, vision, premonition) is accompanied by a corresponding outer physical event which could not have been causally connected with the former. Most cases of extra-sensory perception are considered to be examples of synchronicity.

THINKING. One of the four psychic functions according to Jung. It is the rational capacity to structure and synthesize discrete data by means of categories and conceptual generalizations.

TRANSFERENCE. The emotional involvement, either positive or negative, based on unconscious factors which the patient feels for the psycho-therapist. The transference is due to the projection of unconscious contents onto the therapist.

TRAUMA, PSYCHIC. A damaging psychological experience not readily as-similated consciously. It produces an unconscious complex (*q.v.*) which can be healed only through a reliving (abreaction) of the original experience.

UNCONSCIOUS, THE. That portion of the psyche which is outside conscious awareness. The unconscious expresses itself in dreams, phantasies, obsessive preoccupations, slips of the tongue, and accidents of all kinds. Jung distinguishes two layers of the unconscious: the personal unconscious derived from the personal experience of the individual, and the collective unconscious containing the universal patterns and images called archetypes which are shared by all humans.

Rockingham Public Library

Harrisonburg, Virginia 22801

1. Books may be kept two weeks and may be renewed once for the same period, except 7 day books and magazines.

2. A fine is charged for each day a book is not returned according to the above rule. No book will be issued to any person incurring such a fine until it has been paid.

3. All injuries to books beyond reasonable wear and all losses shall be made good to the satisfaction of the Librarian.

4. Each borrower is held responsible for all books charged on his card and for all fines accruing on the same.